The Armadillo, the Pickaxe, & the Laundry Basket

LORI B. DUFF

This is not a work of fiction. Neither is it a work of fact, at least not entirely. It is mostly true, and mostly harmless. Most people named are who I say they are. Some names and situations have been slightly altered to protect the privacy of the people whose stories I have stolen, more or less always with permission. Some situations have been exaggerated for effect, or tweaked a little bit, because they were funnier the way I tweaked them.

No animals were harmed in the making of this book, except maybe the armadillo, who was mostly just terrified, but many many cups of coffee were drunk.

This book is dedicated to everyone
who bought a copy of the last book, and
especially for those who bought two.

Table of Contents

Waah Waah Waah

Manufactured Emergencies

Back in the olden days, when dinosaurs roamed the Earth, Pangaea was still a continent, and Moses was starting kindergarten -- I'm talking the 1970s and 1980s to hear my kids say it -- very few of us had answering machines. Remember that? Remember when instructing people to leave a message 'after the beep' was actually an instruction some people needed because they'd never left a message on a machine before? No one except the super rich had cell phones, and they were either briefcase sized or tethered to a car. My father, who enjoys talking on the phone about as much as he loves dental surgery, thought the whole cell phone concept was insane. He took the receiver and curly cord off of one of those phones we used to have that was actually connected to the wall, and kept it in his briefcase. Occasionally, while on the commuter train, just to be obnoxious, he would pull it out, trap the cord between the latches of the briefcase, and pretend to have a conversation. In the car, he would stick the cord between the seats. Naturally, this embarrassed the bejeebers out of me and my sister, but we got over it, and now, in retrospect, I think that's kinda funny.

And I also see his point. What is so urgent that it can't wait until I get home or to the office? Nothing. I'm not an emergency responder. In fact, I'm pretty useless in an emergency. Blood and gore ick me out, I admit to a great deal of cowardice when it comes to bad guys, I cannot aim a weapon of any kind in any kind of purposeful direction, and I have never once in my life thrown a real punch. I'm pretty sure I can't take one either. So, if something is truly urgent, the last person you want to summon to the scene is me. Call 911. If it isn't a 911 situation, it isn't an emergency. Period. No arguments.

Not too long ago, I was doing business with someone with whom I do business often, and he stopped our transaction every time his phone made a noise (which was every fifteen seconds) to look and see what the source of the noise was and to occasionally 'text back' or whatever the heck he was doing. I put up with it for a while, and then finally said, "Do you know what happens if you ignore the beep?" He looked at me as if I were about to reveal the location of the Holy Grail.

"No! What?"

I didn't answer right away, making room for a dramatic pause to build tension. "Absolutely nothing."

"But what if it is an emergency?" He said incredulously, as if I'd asked him to completely ignore a young child chasing a litter of puppies into traffic.

"Then whoever is calling you should be calling 911. You are not an emergency responder. Everything and everybody else can wait until we are done here."

"What if someone is dead?"

"Then they will still be dead an hour from now."

Perhaps I am unsympathetic or unfeeling. It wouldn't be the first time someone has accused me of such coldness. But I don't think so. I think this is a matter of common courtesy which, as we all know, is as common as undiscovered Shakespeare plays. In the 45 years of my life so far, there has only been one time that a phone call required my immediate attention, when my husband called me to tell me that my 3 year old daughter had fallen at day care and broken her arm. I flew to the scene of the crime. But the truth is that if I hadn't gotten the call for an hour, her arm would be no differently broken and my husband, who was there, could have competently handled the situation without me. I wanted to be there and I am infinitely glad that I was -- but I didn't *need* to be there in the way that you *need* oxygen and a pumping heart. The outcome would have been the same. If it were still the olden days when pictures were taken on actual film and you had to get off the sofa to change a channel, and I didn't find out until I got home and got the message off the answering machine, or off a scribbled note left on the kitchen table, or even if I'd had to call around to the emergency rooms to find them, everything would have been ok – in fact, exactly the same -- in the end.

The point is this -- be there when your babies need you. Be accessible to your friends and family. Return messages in a timely fashion. But if we are talking to each other, I hope I am interesting enough to distract you from a text message from Chili's offering free chips and salsa. I do like Chili's chips and salsa, though, so if you get one, take me with you. I promise not to double dip.

Breakfast of Champions

My darling husband, who, if you remember correctly, or if you didn't know before hand, is retired and therefore in Charge of Most Things Domestic, does most of our grocery shopping. He is not especially skilled at this seemingly unskilled task, but since he is home and I am not, it has become his job.

He cannot resist a buy one get one free sale. It doesn't matter what it is, or if we want or need it. If it is buy one get one free he will buy four. If it is also new and/or improved, he will buy eight. It is also notable that this is a man old enough to be retired, who lives more or less entirely on Skittles and Smith Brothers Warm Apple Pie Cough Drops. And coffee and beer.

Given that set of starting facts, it should surprise you not at all that he recently came home from his every other day foray into the wilds of Publix with "Hershey's Cookies 'n' Creme" cereal boxes. This was a big hit with all three of my children, both the two who are actually children, and the retired guy with access to keys and a credit card who bought the box. My first thought was "ew," and I said as much out loud. My daughter, who has not yet figured out that advertisers and marketers manipulate facts for their own purposes, defended the purchase by declaring that the box said that whole grain was the first ingredient. This, of course, made me grab the box and see for myself. The first five ingredients were, in order, as follows: whole grain corn, sugar, soybean oil, another kind of sugar (dextrose), and then another kind of sugar (corn syrup). Further on down the list were two other kinds of oil and another kind of sugar. The last few ingredients were a bunch of added vitamins and minerals. The serving size is 3/4 cup which, if I'm not mistaken, is a large handful, which is a good bit less than is normally eaten at one sitting.

So then I went in the pantry and got out a box of our 'compromise' cereal, "Fruity Cheerios" and compared the ingredients. The first five ingredients were: whole grain corn, sugar, whole grain oats, corn syrup (more sugar), and pear puree concentrate. Still a lot of sugar, but no fat and an actual fruit part. The last few ingredients were a similar list of vitamins and minerals.

So I compared the nutritional information. The Cheerios had double the fiber of the Chocolate Frosted Sugar Bombs, which gave it a whopping two whole grams of fiber. The rest of it was virtually the same, except that the Cheerios had a lot more folic acid and half the fat, though the fat was not bad in the other: 3 grams. Ah, those Cheerio marketing people (who, by the way, are the same folks at General Mills corporate headquarters that market the Cookies 'n' Creme cereal.) Fooling parents into thinking you are buying something healthier than Cookies 'n' Creme. It makes you wonder if maybe the only reason why they manufactured the Cookies 'n' Creme in the first place was a) to make the Fruity Cheerios look better by comparison and b) for the stoned (male) college student looking for an easy snack that doesn't require refrigeration or utensils.

Thus frustrated, I pulled out a box of what is referred to as "grownup cereal" in our house, Great Grains.   The front of the box uses words like "less processed," "wholesome," "nutritious," and "fiber rich." The first five ingredients were:

Whole grain wheat, raisins, whole grain rolled oats, dates, and brown sugar. Sounds great, right? TWO kinds of fruit! Brown sugar instead of ultra processed sugar! This is health food, no? Weeellll, hang on. It has more fat and sodium than the Cookies 'n' Creme. It does have five times the fiber, which matters a lot when you are over 40. And four times the protein, which means you are less likely to crash from the sugar high 45 minutes later. But it had less vitamin C and calcium and zinc, and was pretty much the same for everything else. It also has twice the calories.

So what's my point? As usual, I have none. I don't wake up early enough to cook, so cereal is a quick and easy option for us, and is still probably better than a chocolate and marshmallow 'granola' bar. I guess it means I shouldn't fool myself into feeling virtuous by eating the Cheerios. I'll just have Cookies 'n' Creme and crash face first into my coffee by 9:30am. In other words, a typical day.

How to Operate A Refrigerator in Twenty-Six Easy Steps

We recently bought a new refrigerator. Our old one, which I can't quit thinking of as new, was 15 years old, and could only freeze things to "slushie" level, so it was time. The new refrigerator looks like a space-refrigerator. It has blue mood lighting when you open the doors, and touch screen buttons to choose between "ice," "crushed ice," and "water". Lots of things slide and adjust and pull out for your ever changing food storage needs.

But still, it is a refrigerator, and operates as refrigerators have since the invention of iceboxes – you open the door, you put the food in it, and then you close the door. When you want the food back, you open the door, take the food out, and then close the door.

This refrigerator, however, came with a twenty-six page manual. Twenty-six pages (fifty two if you count the Spanish version also in the booklet.) Are there really twenty-six pages of stuff to say about the operation of a refrigerator?

As a lawyer, who deals in stating the obvious in painful detail for a living because there is nothing people can't (and won't) screw up and then sue about later without explicit instruction, I understand that every direction in the manual beyond "Open door, place food inside, close door" comes because of some tragically preventable story. So now I know that if I want my electric refrigerator to be operational, I should plug it in.

I should also not plug it in if my hands are wet, because that might result in a shock. I should take care not to store water in such a way that it might spill all over the electrical workings because that might result in a shock or a fire or perhaps an outbreak of the plague. If I want to turn the icemaker off, I should push the button labeled "Icemaker Off," as it will result in the icemaker being turned off. Thanks for clearing that one up.

There is a two page guide on how long you can keep stuff in your refrigerator or freezer. Apparently this guide was written by the "Buy More Groceries More Often" lobbying group. According to this guide, I can only keep butter in the refrigerator for 2-3 weeks. Citrus fruit can only be kept 1-2 weeks, and ground beef and chicken can only be kept for a day. A day? Are you kidding? That means if my family of American-style carnivores wants to eat meat every day we have to go to the grocery store every day. Sausage, too, can only be kept for 1-2 days. Sausage? For realsies? That stuff is so well cured and salted that you could leave it in the SUN for 1-2 days and be fine with eating it. Seriously, y'all, there's stuff in my fridge that pre-dates the birth of my children, and it hasn't killed me yet. Next they are going to be telling me that I should throw out spices that are more than a decade old. Bwahahahahahha!

There were also some 'helpful' troubleshooting tips. For example, if there were an unpleasant smell in my refrigerator, I should look for food with strong odors, such as old fish. If the food in the refrigerator part starts to freeze, I should check that the temperature is set to above freezing. And, of course, if the whole thing quits working, I should check that it is plugged in.

They say information is power, and I guess that's true, but ignorance is also bliss. I think I was happier eating food until it smelled or looked funny or until the expiration date was two days ago. I was happier thinking that the most complicated thing about my food storage device was figuring out how to shove everything in there without anything spilling or getting lost until it grew a fuzzy green coating.

Speaking of fuzzy green coatings, I sure hope that's a kiwi in there. Whatever. I'm eating it anyway.

Selfies

I read somewhere recently that the good folks at Oxford (I can't remember if it is the dictionary people, the university people, or the shoe people, but in any event it was a name that signified Quality and Serious Business) recently named 2013's word of the year. It is, I am sad to report, "Selfie."

A selfie, for both of you out there who don't know what the word means, is a picture of oneself, taken by oneself. There may or may not be something significant in the background, and there may or may not be another person in the picture. These pictures are then instantly uploaded to Facebook, Twitter, Instagram, or whatever social media I am too middle-aged to know about is the Next Big Thing.

Having viewed gazillions of selfies, and seen a good number of them taken, I know for a fact that there isn't a whole lot of thought behind them, beyond, "*I* need a picture of *me* RIGHT NOW." But they say a whole lot more than that, no matter what the caption says. They say 1) I want a picture of me so badly and so instantly that I'm not going to bother asking someone else to take the picture for me, and 2) I believe deep in my heart that other people out there will not have a complete, fulfilling day until and unless they see a picture of me. Me me me me me me me me me.

Don't get me wrong – one of the reasons why I like social media is that it allows me to keep up with people from my past lives, which includes seeing what they (and their kids) look like now and following their travel and other adventures. I enjoy seeing my friends in Germany during Oktoberfest wearing actual lederhosen. If you just had surgery, I'd like photographic evidence that you came out of it ok. I like your gorgeous family photos; the picture of you pretending to straighten up the Leaning Tower of Pisa as if you are the first person who thought of that perspective joke; and the picture taken moments after your boyfriend proposed while your whole body radiates through the pixels with a happy glow.

What I DON'T need is a way too close close-up picture of you with your eyes cut to the side and the caption, "I'm bored." Oh, are you? Thanks for sharing. Now I'm bored looking at you. "Look! Here I am driving my car!" "Here I am at McDonald's!" "Here I am on line waiting to see the new Hunger Games movie!" Picture me saying 'woo hoo' with the least amount of enthusiasm possible.

As if the basic egotism of these pictures and their public dissemination wasn't enough, lots of them seem to be done in intentionally dumb looking poses. My (least) favorite is the 'duck lips'. In this one, she (it is usually a she) will flatten her smile and poke out her lips to make the best approximation of a duck's bill the human face is capable of without a mask or plastic surgery. No one claims to know where this came from, but I have a theory. Models, with their silicone bee-stung lips, and Botox on the sides of their mouths to prevent both wrinkles and the appearance of genuine pleasure, are often seen in magazines wearing this (supposed to be) brooding, sexy pout. I think duck lips are the 'sexy pout' taken to a ridiculous extreme.

Sometimes I think about what these kids (it is mostly kids who do this – and bear in mind that I consider anyone under

30 a kid) will think of these pictures 25 years from now. As someone who spent all but six months of her teenage years in the 1980s, I am no stranger to embarrassing fashion, hairstyle, and eyewear choices. When my children see some of these pictures, they ask what I was dressed as for Halloween. They can't believe that I looked like that on *purpose*. So part of me laughs for the present, but part of me cringes on behalf of the future of these people who have hundreds of published photographs of themselves looking like something Elmer Fudd is hunting. At least my old, embarrassing pictures are limited to the paper copies in mildewed albums and dry rotted and disorganized negatives.

My daughter, who is on the bottom of the age range for selfie-mania (almost 10), thankfully does not take many. In fact, not too long ago she asked me, "Why do girls take so many selfies? Are they afraid they're going to forget what they look like?" I just laughed when she said that, and didn't give her a real answer, but the truth is that I have one. No, honey, I should have said. They aren't afraid they will forget what they look like. They are afraid that YOU will forget what they look like or who they are unless you are staring at their faces. For a generation whose entire world has an on or off switch, where a social life can come to a screeching halt without an electronic device, and data can be lost in a flash, maybe they think they are no more permanent than the bits and bytes that make up the pictures.

Which begs an existential question: if a person's picture exists in the digital world, and there is no one with their iPod turned on to see it, does the person still exist?

Kids These Days

It wasn't like I was ancient when I had my first child – I was 31 – but I wasn't terribly young, either, and in the neck of the woods where I live the average maternal age is younger than the average maternal age in most of the rest of the country. As a result, I am, if not the oldest, one of the oldest of my kids' friends' Moms.More than once I have found myself at a birthday party relating more to the child's grandmother than their mother. My husband, who is 16 years older than I am, is generally older than the grandparents at the birthday parties.

I say this to tell you that in some ways it makes perfect sense that we would spend a great deal of our time sitting on the front porch in our rocking chairs, making clicking noises with our dentures and shaking our fists at the sky to bemoan the tragedy that is Kids These Days. Our children believe, with good cause, that we are hopelessly uncool, and if we were to even try to be cool it would be worse, because we are way too old for cool, and should just go back to knitting afghans or churning butter or darning socks or whittling pipes out of corn cobs or recounting our latest medical procedures, or whatever it is that old people do to entertain themselves.

As a general rule, I can't stand the television shows my children watch. They are dumb, crude, unfunny, and rude. It is difficult to believe how a person could have ever persuaded a major network to produce and air this dreck, and it truly makes me wonder what horrors were rejected to make air space for such winners as "Stephen Universe," "The Amazing Adventures of Gumball," and "Adventure Time." When I watch these shows, or even catch a glimpse of them, I can hear my brain cells screaming as they jump suicidally from my ears to make the torture stop.

Don't get me wrong – I'm not a prude. I don't really mind some forms of rude and crude so long as it is also clever. But I struggle as a parent what to forbid, what to merely disapprove of, and what I should just chalk up to personal preferences.

And then one day I was flipping through channels on the satellite radio in my car, and happened upon the Broadway channel. After the song I was listening to ended ("One Night in Bangkok" from Chess) the next one to begin was from Bye Bye Birdie. You know the one, the one that starts out, "Kids! What's the matter with kids these days?" It struck me that even back in the allegedly squeaky clean 50s when the Bye Bye Birdie made its debut that people thought that kids these days had just invented being wrong and bad. And then I remembered an essay written a hundred and thirty some odd literal years ago by Mark Twain called "Advice to Youth" that I read a metaphorical hundred years ago. He talks about how kids lie and won't listen to their parents and like to sleep late and are prone to accidental gun violence. But for his frequent use of the word "musket" it could have been written last week.

Then I got to thinking that musical Chess came out when I was roughly my son's age, and some of the lines from One Night in Bangkok are things like, "You're looking at a tourist whose every move's among the purest – I get my kicks above the waistline, Sunshine" and "The Queens we use would not excite you." And how I found a bunch of 25 cent VCR tapes at the local Goodwill of my favorite movies from when I was in Junior High, back before the concept of Middle School was a thing, and bought them for my kids. And was then horrified to be reminded what foul mouthed little kids those Goonies were. I guess I can't go from, "You have to watch this! I know you'll love it! I loved it when I was your age!" to "Oh no, you're not going to listen to this kind of foul language in my house!" in less than ten minutes without appearing like the world's biggest hypocrite and destroying what meager credibility I might have in the future. (They did love it, by the way. Gremlins, too.)

I also thought about how funny I thought it was that people were ever scandalized by the early Beatles, who wore suits and ties and were well groomed and who sang about holding hands. But then, right about the same time the Rolling Stones were singing about how brown sugar tastes so good. Plus, don't forget the Louis Armstrong and Ella Fitzgerald song about how she can't dance with him because she knows good and well she isn't going to stop with just dancing. Or, for that matter, Billy Joel trying to talk poor Virginia out of her virtue.

So, while I will never approve of my kids listening to Ke$ha sing about brushing her teeth "with a bottle of Jack, cuz when she leaves for the night she ain't coming back," I guess I can rest assured that odds are good they'll turn out decently anyway. Theoretically, I have a greater influence on their lives than some pop star they've never met, even if I am their hopelessly dorky Mom.

Money for Movies

The other night I took my children to see the premiere of the movie "The Fault in Our Stars." Ok, I admit it. I took myself to see the premiere. It was only coincidence that my children asked me if they could go before I asked them if I wanted to go, and so I was able to pretend to be the world's coolest and most indulgent Mom when really I was getting my own way.

I'm not really going to talk about "The Fault in Our Stars," so there won't be any spoilers here. However, if you haven't read "The Fault in Our Stars" or seen the movie, I will pause now while you do so, because it is an amazing work of art that appeals to every single person I've ever met, including my generally grouchy husband who only tends to like movies about wars.

Since it was the premiere, and I haven't gone to see the premiere of a movie since Bill Clinton was president, and since everyone under the age of 16 is obsessed with "The Fault in Our Stars," as well as a good number of older folks, I was afraid the movie would be sold out, so I bought tickets online at Fandango. I need to point out here that I rarely go to the movies. It isn't that I don't like going to the movies, or that I don't realize what a completely different experience it is to see something on the big screen with giant speakers coming at you from all directions. It is more that I don't often have four hours in a row with nothing else to do (two hours for the movie, two hours for transportation and finding seats and buying popcorn.) Also, with my kids being relatively young, it is cheaper for me to buy the DVD, since they are going to watch it seventeen jillion times in a row anyway.

But, now that the Dufflets are getting older, and starting to want to watch movies that I might actually want to watch, I guess that is going to change. That is, assuming I get a second job and/or win the lottery. For my standard sized family of four, the tickets cost $40.00. Only one of us is a child, because apparently 12 cycles around the sun passes for 'adult' in buying-movie-ticket land. I don't know about you, but it seems to me that if you aren't technically old enough to watch a PG-13 movie I don't know how you could be defined as an 'adult.' One of us is a senior, but that doesn't matter for jack in terms of pricing. There was a $5.00 'convenience fee.' I don't really have a problem with paying a little extra to buy the tickets this way – I considered it a $5.00 insurance policy that I wouldn't drive all that way only to be disappointed. I just hate the term 'convenience fee,' as if they were charging me $5.00 just to make it easier on me; like the opportunity to give them $5.00 was a favor they only granted me because I was special. I wish they'd be more honest. I wish they'd call it a $5.00 "hey, we've got to make a profit, too" fee.

So we get to the theater, braving weather that, if it were a painting, would be called "The Wrath of God." I'm talking the first born slaying God of Exodus, not any peace and love and forgiveness God. Likely because of the scary weather, and the fact that it was a Thursday and most normal people aren't willing to stay up until midnight on a Thursday, the theater was only about half full.

Because I believe the movie going experience is incomplete without popcorn, we stood on the concession line. For a mere $29.00, we were told, we could buy a plastic bucket of popcorn that was refillable until the end of time for only $3.75 a pop. Figuring I would likely lose (or forget) the bucket before the next time I went to the actual movies, I passed on that bargain. Instead, we got a giant bag o' popcorn and two sodas (just out of curiosity, since movies are shown at night mostly, why are there not more caffeine free options?) for the low low price of $38.00. What? At Publix, an ear of corn is like ten cents. How come it costs ten dollars for an ear's worth of kernels of popcorn? And how much was that again for watered down cola syrup? That's not even getting into the box of Raisinets, which I no longer buy for $5.00 because I have learned that if you buy the big box you get mostly a box, with a tiny little plastic bag inside, maybe the size bag you'd put earrings in from a craft fair, filled with a dozen chocolate covered miniscule raisins. No thanks.

Seriously – if you total what I spent, you outstrip the budget for some lousy movies I saw in the 80s.

Anyway, our wallets thus lightened, we sat down in the theater to watch the commercials on endless loop before the lights dimmed. On time, at 9:30 on the dot, the lights did dim, and the previews began. And didn't hardly end. You wouldn't think there would be so many previews in existence. At 9:54 (really – I checked) we were told that the feature presentation was about to start, but it was a false alarm. Instead, we were treated to a Coke ad disguised as a 'don't we have fabulous surround sound' ad for the theater itself. And a warning to turn our cell phones off.

Eventually, the movie did start, and finish, and it was every bit as heartbreaking and beautiful as the book. It left me sobbing like a baby, trying very hard not to make any noise so as not to bother anyone else or give my children any more fodder with which to make fun of me. I'll tell you what, though – I resent the ridiculous money I spent on the popcorn and soda, but if they had a guy walking around the theater with boxes of tissues like the guys selling beer at a ball game, I'd have gladly forked over the contents of my wallet for the privilege of being able to blow my nose properly.

Grammar Police

I seem to have gotten a reputation as the grammar police. Sometimes I get the impression that people – even my friends, or maybe especially my friends – fear that I am going to rap them on the knuckles with a ruler if they so much as let a single participle dangle.

While it is true that I will judge you for a misplaced apostrophe, and have gone on record as saying so, I won't judge you for the more subtle points of grammar. I am not a grammatical scholar. I read an incredible amount, and always have, and I love words and the way they work. I like the precision that language can produce if you use it properly. I mess it up from time to time, but I try, and theoretically I keep on learning.

No, it is only the things that I think every literate person over the age of 12 should know that I am going to judge you for. (See how I ended that sentence with a preposition? On purpose, no less.) The things for which there can be no argument, and for which there are simple rules. An apostrophe 's' makes a word possessive, not plural. My family is the Duff family. We are the Duffs. If you send us a letter to the Duff's, it will peel back the enamel on my teeth. "They're" means they are. "There" refers to a location that isn't here. "Their" means belonging to them. Always. "It's" means "it is," every single time. "Its" means belonging to it, despite the lack of an apostrophe, and since it is the single exception to that rule, you can go ahead and remember it now.

Also, it is nice to have a verb in a sentence, and somewhere in there should be some kind of indication of who or what is taking the action in that verb.

It also depends upon the context. If you show me a brief you have written to the Supreme Court trying to convince them of the wisdom of your position, you'd better have every comma expertly placed. If you show me a text message you sent from a virtual keyboard while the sun was glaring on the screen and autocorrect was being particularly impish that day, as long as what you wrote is generally comprehensible, it is ok by me.

Typos are not the same as grammatical mistakes. Typos happen. They happen often. I type "teh" nearly as often as I type "the." Given the number of typewritten communications your average grownup is expected to send in any given day, if you stopped to proofread everything you'd never get anything done. You pick the important ones, and fix those. Likewise, spelling errors happen sometimes. I'm not talking about your basic vocabulary words, but words that are semi-common but aren't commonly spelled. Like "diarrhea," which I have to look up every time I spell it, not that I spell it all that often, thank goodness. I can never remember if the word for our local law enforcement guys is Sheriff or Sherrif. (It's Sheriff.) Or if it is personnel or personell. (It's personnel. Don't worry – it isn't personal.)

Frankly, I think anything thumb-typed on a keyboard smaller than the human hand is forgivable. My hands are enormous, and in addition to having thick, manly fingers I also have a movement disorder called essential tremor. This is a mostly benign disorder that makes my extremities shake when the muscles are engaged. Like when I am trying to use my finger muscles to aim directly at tiny buttons the size of Rice Krispies to type letters at a speed that matches the speed of that pterodactyl with a hammer and chisel on the Flintstones. This on top of the fact that autocorrect consistently insists that my daughter's name is "Martin" and that a commonly uttered expression of mine indicating shock and surprise is "Hot Danny!"

Also, I'm aware that I am a big fat nerd. I'm proud of this fact, but I also recognize that nerd-speak can be socially off-putting. So a lot of times, when I'm talking (and in many contexts I consider writing 'talking') I purposely use more casual grammar so that I don't sound like the prig it is very easy for me to sound like. "The green one is the one about which we were talking" makes me sound like I drink tea every day at three pm precisely with my pinky dutifully held high in the air as I look down my nose at the common folk. "The green one is the one we were talking about" makes me sound more like a normal human.

I tell you this not necessarily so that you know that I'm not judging you for saying "me" instead of "I" or for ending a sentence with a preposition. (As Winston Churchill once said to make the point I was making in the above paragraph, "Poor grammar is a habit up with which I will not put.") No, I'm telling you this to take the pressure off me, so I will quit getting triumphant emails from people who have 'caught' me making a mistake.

It happens. (Not happen's. That should never happen.)

Addressing Etiquette

Near the end of October, my son is becoming a Bar Mitzvah, and we are having a reception after the ceremony that has completely gotten out of control. I get that it is essentially a birthday party for a 13 year old boy, but considering the DJ and photographer and formal invitations, it is more like a wedding – the full blown, she-planned-it-since-she-was-a-little-girl type. Add to the mix that my son is the first boy to have a Bar Mitzvah ceremony in about 20 years in my family, and you have one potent cocktail.

No pressure.

Recently, we sent out the invitations. The invitations just might be the most stressful thing I have had to deal with in recent years, and this includes jury trials, broken bones, surgeries, and illnesses that people die of. Picking out the invitations was easy. It got to crunch time, and I forced Jacob to sit with me at the computer for (what I thought was to be) a long evening of combing through websites for ideas. I pulled up one site with about 200 Bar Mitzvah invitation ideas. He pointed to a blue one and said, "I like that one," and walked away. He was done. In two years, I expect the same process will take two weeks with my daughter. That was the last easy part, though.

First of all, the guest list itself was a mess. Who do you invite? This is, after all, a 13 year old's birthday party. It is his show. So his friends, yeah. But which of his friends' parents? How about their younger or older siblings? What about my friends? What about my friends whose kids my son doesn't care for? (No, of COURSE I don't mean your kids – I mean those other kids. The unlikeable and unpleasant ones.) What about the relatives he doesn't know, or even know of? Balance that with the fact that I believe that sending an invitation can easily be seen as a "send my son a gift" notice, and I don't want to force people to give him a gift if I know they can't come. There is no doubt that despite putting the list together for the better part of two months that I left off someone critical, and someone's feelings will get hurt. So know this: I want to invite everyone. I do. But at 50 bucks a head I can't. And you? You were actually invited, only the invitation got lost in the mail or was undeliverable as addressed.

Why? You ask. Why was it undeliverable as addressed? Well, partly it is because I had this moronic idea that hand addressing the envelopes (as opposed to mail-merge address labels) would be more personal. Once upon a time I took calligraphy classes. I know there are those felt tip pens with the slant on the tip where if you just write marginally neatly it can look like calligraphy. I can *do* this, I thought. Why not?

My children both have relatively neat handwriting, and I also figured that my son could do a good bit of the addressing himself. I unearthed some of my old calligraphy practice books, gave him a pen, and told him to practice. His sister wanted to practice, too. Jacob immediately told her that she could not address any invitations, because it was HIS Bar Mitzvah and he didn't want her to participate. This made her really really want to. So I told her she could do her own friends' envelopes.

And so we began. I very quickly learned that, along with cursive, they no longer teach schoolchildren how to address an envelope. We didn't exactly have too many extra envelopes, and it took me too long to realize that they didn't know to put the address in the center of the envelope, or that the name went first; then the street address on the next line; nor that the city, state, and zip, in that order, went on the third line. Some of them I just left, if the name was legible and the zip code was obviously a zip code.

They also didn't know standard conventions about how to address married couples or families. The whole Mrs. Ms. Miss conundrum was a mystery to them. I remember learning all this mess back in my English class (back when it was called an English class, and not 'language arts') sometime in the late 1970's. There were, however, a number of conventional problems that Mrs. Roth never taught me: What do you do when there are three last names within a family? (Her maiden name, his last name, and the kids' father's last name.) What do you do with the lesbian couple who has the same last name? The lesbian couple with different last names and whose kids hyphenate? With the couple that is separated but not divorced? The divorced couple that shares custody – do the kids get invited from both addresses? What about when she is a doctor but he isn't? To be honest, I got tired of trying to figure it all out and took my best guess at some of it. ("The Smith Family," for example, even though her last name isn't Smith, and her other kid, who is invited, has the last name of Jones because he has a different dad and, well, because my head hurts, and if you're my friend and want to partake in the Festive Meal you'll just shake your head at my laziness and forgive me.)

Eventually, we got them all addressed. My daughter, after her hard fought and won battle to participate in the addressing party, addressed all of two envelopes before deciding that it was not only work, but boring thankless work at that. She wandered off to watch episodes of "Cake Boss" on Netflix and was no more help.

Then we had to stuff them. I thought we had a pretty nifty assembly line system, until we realized that approximately every other envelope my son stuffed had a response card but no reply envelope. After several deep breaths, we held the envelopes up to the light and felt them for appropriate thickness before carrreeeeeefulllllllyyyyyy opening the envelopes and retaping them with the proper contents inside. I was fairly angry at his carelessness, but then we compromised and decided that I wouldn't be mad any more if he let me write about his boneheadedness.

Joke's on him, though. The thank you notes haven't even begun yet.

Fiverrrrrr

Let us get one thing straight: I am a capitalist. I believe deep in the recesses of my heart that if you can convince someone to pay for something that you can do, more power to you. And if you can convince them to pay double, well, double the power.

Recently, I needed a simple task done that I didn't have the skill set to do (create a logo) and my friend Suzen of Omaginarium Marketing suggested that I try "Fiverr" because even if it stunk, I'd have only lost five dollars. I had no idea what Fiverr was. Suzen knows a lot of things that I don't know about stuff like that, which is why I ask her those questions. Anyway, Fiverr turns out to be this website (www.fiverr.com) in which people offer their services for five dollars.

The services vary. You can have someone design a logo or a post card, write a letter, edit a letter, or, really anything you can think of. And when I say anything you can think of, I mean anything you can think of. One man offered to rub chocolate on his belly and sing happy birthday in a video. Another man offered to write your message on a beach in Jamaica. Several people were willing to be my Facebook girlfriend for a week (or more!) to make other people jealous.

This is the kind of thing that endlessly fascinates me. I get why people would sell services for five dollars. They need to practice. They need to build their portfolios. They are unemployed and have nothing else to do. My guess is that if you have a lot of these things set up on your computer, it only takes you five or ten minutes to do what you are being asked to do, which works out to $60 an hour, which ain't a bad living if you can get that many takers.

I get the impression that a lot of these things are things that people would do for free only, hey – if I can get a random stranger to give me five bucks to do it, why not? Like the plethora of guys who do a good Morgan Freeman or Christopher Walken impression and will record any message you want in the celebrity voice for $5.

Seriously – would you not spend $5 to have a cashew tree planted in Guatemala in someone's name? What a great birthday gift! I mean, maybe not as good as the video of the creepy clown singing happy birthday, but for that little bit of cash you can buy both!

So that made me think. I mean, everyone has a price. What ridiculous thing would I be willing to advertise on the internet that I'd do for five dollars? Also, what kind of self-confidence does it take to assume that someone, somewhere might actually pay good cash money to have a video of you in an aluminum foil hat wearing nothing but a pair of tube socks and balloons in strategic places?

I'm truly afraid that my children will find out about this. They will do anything that doesn't involve cleaning, folding laundry, or yard work for five dollars.

I also wonder how sincere some of these people are. Eighteen people bought and positively rated the "I will meditate on your love life for twenty minutes" service. Apparently, concentrated thoughts about a perfect stranger's love life are a) worth something to someone; b) specifically, $15 an hour; and c) fill a hole in the market that couldn't be found elsewhere.

It has never once occurred to me to fork over money for someone else to think really hard about my love life. And I wonder if the meditator is really thinking about the meditatee, or just buying some pizza and beer with the meditation money and hoping against hope that karma isn't real.

People really do pay money for this kind of thing. Four hundred some odd people paid some guy to "be the secret admirer they NEVER wanted." That's $2,000.00, assuming no one bought any of the add-ons, which include $20.00 for a personalized birthday wish.

So. What would you do for five dollars? What would I do for five dollars? What would you like to see me do for five dollars? (No. No no no no no. I won't do that.)

My Life

The Armadillo, The Pickaxe, And The Laundry Basket

My brain was full and my body was tired, that's the only way to describe it. It had been a long week at work, the morning was spent doing yard work with my son, and the afternoon was spent swimming and playing in the lake. I disengaged from my family relatively early, about 9:45 pm, and lay down on my bed to read a book. Ahhhhhhhh.

I heard an annoying scratching noise from the direction of the window. At first I thought it was a critter of some kind scratching at the siding. But it didn't quit, and sounded a little scrapier. I finally decided that it was my husband, mucking around in the dark with the bucket and rake I knew he left resting against the house outside our bedroom window. So I got out of bed with the complicated plan to press my face against the window to a) see what exactly he was doing in the dark; and b) knock on the window loudly or shout to startle him. This is the kind of adult fun I like to have.

I walked around to the other side of the bed. As I got to the window, I saw a stick poking up through the air conditioning vent on the floor. The stick was moving, and the vent cover was ajar. My husband had been talking about trying to slither under the crawl space to see if the air conditioning condensation line was full. It is entirely in keeping with my husband's personality to attempt this at night, with a back injury, so I can't be blamed for immediately jumping to the conclusion that it was my husband underneath the house trying to see if there was a blockage of some kind.

And then I saw the armadillo. He was standing right next to the vent, looking up at me, about the size of your average housecat, only armor plated.

Now I know that when I am given the choice of 'fight or flight' I run like hell, screaming, "Mike! Mike! Miiiiiiiiiiike!" Mike was in the kitchen with the kids, and some part of my lizard brain decided that if I stood on the citrus colored striped carpet (I think it appeals to me because it reminds me of Fruit Stripe Gum from the 70s) I would be safe. "There's an armadillo in the bedroom. It came up through the air conditioning vent. I thought it was you messing around outside, but it was an armadillo coming up through the vent."

Mike immediately flew into action, not even pausing to jump into a phone booth to change into his Superman uniform or question the ridiculousness of my story. He high tailed it into the bedroom, with the kids on his heels, both of them giggling and loading up the camera function on their iPods. "Stay back!" he yelled, totally in Protector of the Family mode, and went in the bedroom to do battle, slamming the door behind him. I stayed on the magic carpet, the brain-scrambling adrenaline still telling me I would be safe as long as I remained on the tropical fruit colored stripes.

Mike came back out and announced that he had it trapped in the bathroom and needed all our help. He got a fishing net, designed to scoop up enormous catfish; a pickaxe; and a laundry basket. I stayed on the magically protective carpet until I was called out by name, and even then left its comforting force field with trepidation. I went into the bedroom and hopped up on the center of the bed for safety. The bed wasn't as good as the striped carpet, but it will do.

"I need you to be back up," Mike said, shaking the laundry basket at me. "If he comes running out of the bathroom I need you to throw this on top of him."

"Not me," I said, in a powerful display of cowardice. "I'm staying right here."

Thankfully, my children are not weenies like I am. They fought for the right to wield the laundry basket.

With the net in his right hand and the pickaxe in his left, my brave, brave man went into the bathroom to do battle with the armadillo. At first his voice was soothing. "Come here, little guy. I won't hurt you. Don't be scared." There was a lot of thumping, and the voice devolved from pre-k teacher at naptime to Marine with a Vengeance. "Get out here, you little [expletive deleted] – I swear I will kill you. Get the [expletive deleted] away from the toilet!" More banging and scratching and thumping sounds.

This made my kids start screaming, "Don't kill it! Just bring it outside!" and me start screaming, "Don't kill it in the bathroom! I don't want to clean armadillo guts out of the bathroom!" This made poor Mike start screaming at us to shut up. We shut up. We are not stupid.

Eventually the bathroom door swung open, and the conquering hero stood there with his foot on the tail of the arma-

dillo, its body trapped under the net. "Get me the laundry basket. And some thick towels." Like a seasoned surgical nurse, I brought him what he needed. He threw the towels over the net which was over the armadillo, and wrestled with it to get it into the laundry basket. It was a feisty bugger, and stronger than you'd think a thing like that could be, so Mike held onto it in the basket, and slid the basket across the floor and down the hallway over to the back door in a position you might call the "Downward Facing Armadillo," the whole time shrieking for us to get in front of him and open the back door.

He managed to get everything outside, uncovered the armadillo, and it ran off, not before getting an ineffectual kick on the rear of its armored plates to make sure it ran off away from the house.

It took a while to clean up the mess, disinfect the bathroom and bedroom carpet and make sure all the air conditioning vents were secure in case Octivian (my daughter's name for the armadillo) told his friends about his great adventure and they wanted to duplicate it. It also took a while to get our heart rates to a healthy rate and calm down enough to go to sleep.

It's always something, isn't it?

Angry Resting Face

I need to come clean on something. I suffer from a condition that until recently I didn't know had a name until a friend of mine named it and claimed to be a fellow sufferer. It is called "Angry Resting Face." (Feel free to replace the word 'angry' with the descriptor of your choice. The one suggested to me was considerably less family friendly.) Apparently, when I am not struck by any particular kind of emotion, or aware of the things that my facial muscles are doing, the default position of my facial demeanor is angry looking. My mouth, when slack, curves downward, making it look like I am frowning. My eyes are naturally rather small (though not, I think, beady) and when I am not making an effort to keep them open they appear to be narrowed into little slits. The fact that as I age my eyelids are doing their best to droop down further and further over my eyes does not help this situation.

If I am Deep In Thought, it is much worse. Like some people might squint their eyes in order to better focus their sight on something, apparently I squint my eyebrows in order to better focus my brain on something. They nudge themselves together, resulting in the typical cartoon downward-and-inward slant of someone trying to execute her plot to take over the world. (Seriously, though. If I did take over the world, wouldn't it be a much better place?) The wrinkles this eyebrow slanting creates on my forehead and between my eyes only heightens the effect. My unibrow, which is usually but not always tamed by painful waxing, can send the look over the edge.

As a lawyer, this can sometimes work to my advantage. When I am in the courtroom, I am thinking constantly, and so my inadvertent game face has gotten me called a number of mean things that work in my favor when doing battle. Image can be everything. Don't mess with me, this face says: I will hurt you and possibly slash the tires of your car if you do. Although what I am probably thinking is, "Oooh! Arby's just reintroduced the Orange Cream Milkshake!"

People who only know me in the courtroom, then, don't really know me at all. Many years ago, when my children were little bitties, I was talking in the hallway of a Courthouse about something especially cute my especially cute children did. One of the Courtroom deputies standing nearby heard me, and looked me deep in the eyes as if she were trying to take measure of my soul. "You have kids?" she asked in the same tone she would have used to ask about my third head.

"Yes," I said, immediately jumping from lawyer mode to gushing mommy mode, extolling the virtues of the world's most perfect, adorable, and intelligent babies.

She looked at me with her jaw hung low. The same "what rabbit hole have I fallen down?" look she would have given her dog if it had suddenly asked her the square root of 2209. (The answer is 47, by the way. The calculator told me, not the dog.) "You have kids," she said slowly, testing the words for accuracy as they came out of her mouth. "Huh. I would have thought you were too mean to have children."

I alternatively think this is hilarious and sad. It explains some social problems I had when I was in school. The first time I ever became aware of it I was a senior high school, and a boy whose social status was far higher than mine informed me that people were scared of me. Given that, at the time, I was scared of almost everyone and everything in a social setting, I was flabbergasted. "Why?" I asked.

"Because people are afraid you are going to bite their heads off if they say something wrong."

Ok, I admit to having some revenge fantasies about biting people's heads off if they say something especially stupid, but I would never ever in a thousand years actually do it. I think of myself as a pretty even keeled person, who is quick to laugh, slow to anger, and is always looking to make a joke. I probably don't take most things seriously enough. Frankly, I think that in addition to Angry Resting Face that I also suffer from Pseudobulbar Affect which is a real, live, actual, and true neurological condition which occurs in 11% of the people who have the other neurological condition I have actually been diagnosed by a real doctor with, Essential Tremor. Anyway, one of the main symptoms of Pseudobulbar Affect is that you laugh uncontrollably in inappropriate situations, like funerals and business meetings. Ummmmmm, guilty.

In the meantime, I will use my Angry Resting Face to my advantage when I can. Maybe I'll start a foundation and have a telethon featuring some actor with an angry looking face who is actually very funny in real life. (Christopher Walken? Clint Eastwood? Robert DiNiro?) We'll sell those rubber bracelets in some angry looking swirl of colors like black, red, and puke green, with a slogan like, "Angry Face = Happy Heart." We can have Angry Resting Face Awareness week in elementary schools and booths at craft fairs where we sell pastries that look disgusting but taste delicious. The possibilities are endless.

Now, if you'll excuse me, I have to practice smiling in the mirror. I'm volunteering at the elementary school next week, and I only want to scare kids off if I mean to.

To Sleep...Perchance To Dream

Despite my complicated relationship with it, I like to sleep. I mean, I like to sleep in the way that most people like indoor plumbing and oxygen. This isn't something that has always been the case, and I don't know what has changed, other than, well, I guess the obvious (age and motherhood) but it is what it is.

When I was in high school, we lived in a small house and only had one shower and a limited hot water tank. All four of us wanted to take a shower in the morning, and so to ensure that I could get much needed bathroom time and not have to rinse my hair (which was long and plentiful at the time) in ice water I woke up at 5:00 am to take the first shift. I considered myself a 'morning person' and was fully functional from the moment I became conscious. I actually liked the quietness of the early morning before most people were up. As a small child I remember being the first one up and wondering why every-one else just wanted to lie in bed and do nothing. My Mother was at the absolute other end of the spectrum, and it was the job of me and my sister to make sure she woke up in time to get to work. This was always something we dreaded doing. At first she'd groan things like, "just five more minutes" but when we got more urgent she'd say things through gritted teeth like, "if you bother me one more time I will put my elbow in your eye."

In college, I convinced myself that I didn't need much sleep – or maybe I really didn't back then. I remember a time when there was no point in going to a party/event/club until 11:00 pm because nothing happened before then, and also thinking that was not only reasonable but do-able. I remember studying until about 1:00 am, and then going to bed and setting my alarm for 4:00 am to finish what I hadn't gotten done. As long as I got at least three hours of sleep in a row I figured I'd had a good night's sleep. Of course, that was back in the day where in the Student Center there were couches and chairs (and hideously ugly lamps that were welded to the side tables as if someone were in danger of saying, "I must have that horrible lamp!" and stealing it) all over the place. There were generally people in the couches and chairs sleeping, sometimes with notes pinned to their shirts saying something like, "If I'm still sleeping at 4:30, please wake me." I was occasionally (ok, often) one of those people.

These days if I am in not in my PJs by 9:30, you know something has gone terribly wrong. If I know ahead of time I am only going to get six or seven hours of sleep I dread the next day, which I know will be a yawn-fest and a real slog to get through. I know for a fact I'm not nearly as quick-witted or able to think on my feet when I'm tired. When the alarm rings it gets snoozed within an inch of its life, and I really truly am not functional until I've had a cup (or three) of coffee and some time to clear my head.

All of this might lead you to the conclusion that I am *good* at sleeping, but that's not true, either. Without the aid of modern medicine, I sleep only intermittently and very shallowly. There are many nights in which I am convinced I didn't sleep at all. I have contrived elaborate sleep rituals to try to combat this – glass of milk, reading, lavender oils – but they only work a little. I did a sleep study once upon a time to see if there was any physiological reason why this was (there wasn't.) Of course, if I have trouble sleeping in my own bed, you can only imagine how much trouble I have in a strange bed, especially with about seventy zillion wires glued to different spots all over my body, and with the knowledge that there was someone I had only just met watching me on a monitor all night. I don't remember the exact number, but after that event I learned that I had something like only 63% sleep efficiency, which was relatively stinky on the scale of sleep efficiency.

I'm always surprised after a big [insert exhausting event like birthday party/trial/wedding/performance here] when people want to go out afterwards for a cup of coffee or glass of wine to celebrate and/or console themselves. All I ever want (even without the excuse of a big event) is a nap. Probably because I so rarely get them. It makes me stamp my feet like a three year old about the fact that actual three year olds complain about being forced to take naps.

So here's my proposal. We should make some kind of regulation, or at the very least make it a social norm, that around 3:00pm every afternoon we are in a state called "quiet time" and we all have to speak in whispers and/or put our heads down on our desks and just chill for a half hour. Kind of like tea time, but without the caffeine, fine china, and crumpets. I honestly think productivity would go up.

Now, if you'll excuse me, it is getting on 9:00pm as I type this, and it is time for me to get my glass of milk.

All Wrapped Up

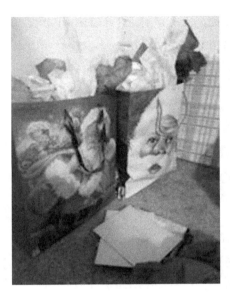

Somewhere near the top of the list of Things that Require Physical Coordination that I am incapable of doing is wrapping presents. As this is December as I write this, there are a lot of presents to be wrapped.

The easy answer is gift bags. Gift bags have a lot to recommend them. They can be made to look attractive by (almost) anyone, and are easy to use and reusable until the seams start to split or until someone thoughtlessly puts a non-removable "To: Lori From: Your Best Friend Ever" sticker in an obvious place over the decorations. Of course, nine times out of ten when I personally use a gift bag, I can't make the tissue paper look all cute and poufy like everyone else can. It looks as if I've wadded the tissue up after using it for a housekeeping task and then lobbed it from across the room at the bag. The other downside is that when keeping presents around children for a gift giving occasion to occur Not Right This Minute, it is awfully easy to peek around the tissue paper and see what is in it. It is hard to keep a surprise in an easily accessible package.

So, I'm stuck with using wrapping paper. Also, I have about 86 million billion kajillion rolls of wrapping paper because my children, and all my friend's children, sell over priced wrapping paper each year as a fundraiser for the PTO and I feel obligated to buy anything children are selling. Furthermore, the joy of tearing up wrapping paper is inextricably a part of the fun of getting a present.

I try. I really do try. In theory, I do know how to do this. I know to cut the paper the length of the two long and two short sides of the box. I know to leave enough on the sides to cover the sides. I know to pull it as tightly as I can so it doesn't look loose and rumply. I know to use the tape the long way so as to maximize the sticking. I know to fold over the edges and tuck them underneath and pull up the flap. Still, the end result always looks as if I wrapped the present in the dark. With my toes.

And, God forbid the present isn't a square or rectangle. I have to smush the wrapping paper on and quickly fling a strip of tape on to hold it long enough for me to get the six or seven other strips of tape on that will hold the whole thing together. I usually have to get scraps of wrapping paper to fill in the holes inevitably left by my crooked wrapping job. Although I don't usually bother with ribbons on rectangular presents, I do have to use ribbons on oddly shaped presents, or they are likely to be picked up and thrown out with the balled up wrapping paper scraps they look like. Plus, if you tie it all around the package in at least two different directions, it is more likely to stay intact.

I feel badly about this, though I know I shouldn't. I really do appreciate the artistry that goes in to a present wrapped using hospital corners with a bow that matches the wrapping paper.   When I do use a bow it is usually one I found on the floor of the coat closet and I have to pick off dust bunnies and stray pieces of schmutz from the used up sticky part.   Then I have to figure out a way to get it to stick on the present without the use of the original stickum and without getting tape all over the place which is another esthetical disaster to go along with my lousy wrapping job.

I do, however, think I am pretty good about picking out what goes IN the present.   Of course, probably everyone thinks they are, even the ones who give you the stuff that immediately goes into the closet everyone has in their houses for re-gifting.   In theory, it is what is in the present that matters.   The thought behind the gift: that you were in a store and thinking of your friend/relative/coworker/secret Santa recipient when you said, "This.   Of all the things in this store or any other, this is what will make her happy."   Or fulfill my obligation.   Or whatever.

In sum, friends, and other recipients of the thoughtful crap I've bought all year and stored away until the appropriate gift giving occasion came around: please.   Judge me by the gift, not the package it came in.   Unless you don't like the gift, either.   In which case, just smile and say thank you and give it to someone else who might like it better.   I'm ok with that.

Serving Cheetos in A Tiffany Bowl

When my first book, Mismatched Shoes and Upside Down Pizza, came out, I was asked to read chapters of it at certain events. I am thrilled to do this, mainly because I think it will be easy to guilt everyone in the room into buying a copy. It is a lot harder to look me in the eye and say, "no" than it is to ignore my self-aggrandizing, begging and pleading and pitiful Facebook posts and other marketing attempts. These 'readings' forced me to ask the question, "What chapter should I read?" Honestly, I have not ever counted the chapters in the book, and they are not numbered (note to self: count them one day soon so I will have an answer when people ask), but I would guess there are about fifty of them, all just a few pages long. Each one is my baby, and I cannot make any Sophie's Choices about which is my favorite. So I asked my friends.

As things tend to do in my life, that question took on a life of its own, which ended up in a small get-together at my house, featuring Cheetos and Wine and me reading the suggested chapters to see how they went over out loud. If you don't know why Cheetos and Wine play into this, you haven't read my book and, well, pooh on you for that. I will pause for a moment while you go get it and read it.

My children and I did a blitz-cleaning of the house prior to the Cheetos and Wine mini-impromptu party, stuffing as much detritus as we could into closets that were unlikely to be opened, picking up the dust bunnies large enough to qualify as dependents on my taxes and shooing them into the yard, and stacking the rest into piles we hoped would be considered neat and purposeful. I actually looked up online which wine would pair best with Cheetos, and ended up buying a Pinot Noir, a screwtop Riesling, two bottles of Grape-Juice-In-A-Wine-Bottle, and a large bag each of puffed and crunchy Cheetos. I also bought some crackers and grown-up looking cheese so I could pretend to have also served some real food to my guests.

 Back in the day when I was engaged, and had the ability to register for things that I would never in a zillion years buy for myself, I registered for several crystal bowls. My mother always had a few of these bowls in the house, and under the theory of "why have them if you aren't going to use them?" would fill them with whatever needed to be put in a bowl. So naturally I reached for the Tiffany bowl with the hearts on it for the crunchy Cheetos, and the Lenox tulip bowl for the puffy. I put the cheese on a silver plated tray. Aside from the fact that these bowls each cost more than some of the furniture in my house, they are very practical bowls. The clear lead crystal displays the contents nicely. They are easy to clean. There are high walls that make sure your Cheetos will stay in the bowl. Plus, they each weigh about 35 pounds (no, seriously) and are virtually impossible to knock over, no matter how many tweenage children are flinging couch pillows around the room at each other. They are stunningly beautiful, very practical pieces.

There is something profound about this juxtaposition that I haven't quite worked out, or maybe it is just a hands-on example of what my life has become. I like to think it is a matter of pride (not a matter of low class shame) that I think nothing of serving lowly Cheetos in a bowl whose value is greater than the GDP of some developing countries. Who says delicious, delicious Cheetos are not as deserving of a pretty bowl as some nasty mush made from the liver of a force fed duck? I'm at home with all of it, and I like that about me, even if you do think it is tacky. A college friend of mine said that it was a mark of true style to be able to combine high and lowbrow items with panache. I don't know if she meant it (she is, by profession, a world-renowned psychologist, and therefore accustomed to making people feel better about their foibles), or was just trying to find an excuse to use 'panache' in a sentence, but I'm gonna take it and run with it.

I do this sort of thing all the time. My go-to dish for a pot-luck is always a box of 50 assorted Munchkins from Dunkin Donuts. People laugh at me when I bring them in their conveniently-handled cardboard box, comparing their high rent casserole with the wilted spinach leaves lovingly baked to my fried-and-sugared-by-a-stranger dough, but guess which one of us never takes home leftovers? Just this very day I went to a potluck luncheon at my Synagogue, where most of the participants were retired Jewish Mothers. Jewish Mothers are notorious for their desire to shove food down the throat of every problem and use it to celebrate every victory. My people can cook, and there was a smorgasbord of casseroles and stews and salads and other kinds of yumminess. I brought my Munchkins, which, for extra added tacky, were handed to me through the drive-thru window in a box decorated with Christmas Trees (this is late February as I type this.)

As far as I know, no one noticed. But every single person ate Munchkins.

To paraphrase that arbiter of good taste and the je ne se quoi that makes the good life so very good, Larry the Cable Guy, I don't care who you are. That's good stuff right there.

Before I had finished working out this existential crisis, my friends came over, along with a few of my children's friends (my book is G rated, by the way, with a few forays into PG, thoroughly vetted by a friend whose idea of strong language is "dangit!" and who cringed in horror at the chapter about my son's obsession with flatulence) and we ate Cheetos and actual cheese and drank our varieties of grape juice before the reading began.

My husband Mike is usually a wanderer, hence his nickname "Waldo[1]," and can't stay put in a room. So it didn't shock me at all when he walked out of the back door during the party carrying a spotlight and a stick, announcing that he was going to 'chase turkeys.' It did surprise some of my friends who weren't that familiar with him, and when they crunched their eyebrows together to make that "What the ....?????" face, I just rolled my eyes towards the attic and shook my head. Seriously, don't ask me about the stupid wild turkeys spotted in

---

[1] We never know where he is and inevitably someone asks where he might be. Our pat response is, "I don't know, Where's Waldo?" Sadly, I have yet to convince him to wear a red and white striped rugby shirt and hat on Halloween.

the back yard and which chased my son in a drama he swears "nearly killed" him, despite the fact that they have leeeeeeetle bitty legs, can't fly well, and my son used to run track. Not well, mind you, but run he did.

Most of the time, I think I'm a pretty good wife. I mean, I'm not Donna Reed or Mrs. Cleaver or anything, I don't have dinner waiting when he gets home, or vacuum with my pearls on. Not that those things necessarily define a good wife these days anyway, if they ever did. But I am loyal, I take care of him when he is sick, and generally don't give him half the grief he deserves. But I really dropped the ball last Saturday night.

At some point Mike came back in from the Great Turkey Adventure, and pulled me aside with an, "I need to talk to you" spoken with quite some seriousness and urgency. I excused myself, followed him into our bedroom, where he promptly stripped off his shirt to show me that he was covered in hives. "I'm reacting to something," he said.

"No duh," I said, helpfully. "What is it?"

"I don't know."

"Take a Benadryl," I said and then walked back into the living room to be hostess to my guests. This sort of thing happens on rare occasions to him, and Benadryl generally clears it up, so I didn't think I was being terribly unsympathetic. I went on and read my chapters, my friends and I debated the reactions of the room to the readings, and we made a decision. (If you want to know what I decided, you'll just have to invite me to your book club/church group/community service organization/etc.) I went back to check on Mike. I stuck my head in the bedroom. "Are you ok?" I called. "YeaBLURGHHHHH!" I heard, and

I felt my own bile rising dangerously in my throat. Between heaves, I understood that he had taken two tablespoons of some Ipecac in an effort to rid himself of whatever was triggering the reaction. Expired Ipecac. But, he figured, what harm could Ipecac that expired during the first Gulf War do? Would it make you *not* throw up?

I'm not good with bodily fluids of any kind. I'm just not good with that. Nope. I used to be better about it when my children were babies. There was nothing that leaked out of their very leaky bodies that I wouldn't handle with aplomb. That includes the time when my one year old son was sitting on my lap to try on shoes at Stride Rite and he suddenly hurled and my instinct was to cup my hands in front of his mouth to catch it all so as to save the carpeting and furniture in the store. (I did, by the way, which then led to some interesting logistical questions, such as how to get the crying, sick baby off my lap without spilling, and what to do with the contents in my hands while making the least amount of mess possible and not causing anyone else to join in.)

So, given the fact that there really wasn't anything useful for me to do, and the last thing we needed was both grownups who lived in the house tossing cookies around the bathroom while we had company, I said, "tell me if you need anything," and went back to my friends. I checked on him periodically and extremely briefly. I'm pretty sure he purged himself of a lunch he ate while JFK was still president, and the heaving lasted well into the night. The hives went down before the guests left, and so I went to bed at my normal time, under the theory that there was nothing I could do for him, as his hair is short and I don't need to hold it out of the way for him, and our kids needed at least one functional parent, which wasn't going to be the case if I stayed in the room with him.

I have since learned that they neither manufacture nor sell Ipecac anymore, and it is specifically contra-indicated.

So yeah. I was a pretty lousy wife that night. But I think he's forgiven me, even if he won't eat Cheetos anymore.

An Ode To Coffee

My friend Sheri said this to me the other day: "I like going to bed at night because it means I can wake up and drink coffee." This, I thought, was one of the more profound things anyone has said to me in the history of ever. It hit me at my source.

Ok, ok, ok. I know. There are some of you out there that don't like coffee. This is incomprehensible to me. Coffee isn't just a beverage. Coffee is a sensual experience, a ritual, the fuel that keeps America running and makes this country great, despite the fact that to my knowledge not a single bean is grown on continental American soil. I'm generally an open minded person, and I like having friends of different backgrounds and races and religions because they are interesting to me. But I admit a prejudice: if you don't drink coffee, I think there is something suspicious about you, and I will never fully trust you. Ha ha. I'm just kidding. Sort of.

Nutritional studies seem to be all over the map, at least according to that most credible of sources, Facebook. Coffee is good for you. Coffee is bad for you. Coffee dehydrates you. Coffee is just as good as water for hydration. Coffee stains your teeth. Coffee regulates your bowels. Whatever. If the internet experts can't agree, I'm not going to weigh in, except to say that I strongly believe in the studies that say it is good for you.

I may be a little extreme in my love for coffee, but I know that Sheri and I are not alone. I have another friend who started roasting his own coffee in his backyard because he couldn't find satisfaction elsewhere, and the results cannot be compared. He has since turned this into a nifty little business. (Thanks Steve from Trinity Coffee Roasters – do I get some free coffee for the unsolicited plug?) His coffee is so fresh and so good that I have accused him of importing cocaine as well as coffee beans from Colombia because there is so much buzzy caffeine in some of the varieties.

Which brings me to the inspiration for this little ode to coffee. A few days ago, I had a migraine. The horrible kind (not that there is a unicorn and rainbows kind) that doesn't get knocked right out with medication and eventually results in nausea and the losing of one's breakfast/lunch/dinner. This happened once in a Judge's Chamber during a pretrial conference, which is a story for another day. (Note to self: does my family find itself experiencing reverse peristalsis more than most families, or do we just speak of it publicly more often?) Usually when this happens, I go to sleep and when I wake up I am mainly functional, and by the next day I'm ok.

Only now it is the day after the next day and I'm still not ok. My headache has gone away, even though there are still the occasional aftershocks. But my stomach has not gotten back to normal. Most food does not appeal to me, and even plain drinks like water make me a little queasy. The only things I have been able to consume with any gusto are Coke Zeros and Ritz Crackers. So, part of me thinks, "weeee hooooo!" Diet by illness – whatever, so long as it works, right? But the other part of me wakes up in the morning and pours coffee in the cup and smells it and waits for the endorphin rush triggered by the dark, earthy smell and anticipation of the complex flavors and stimulant rush of the caffeine. Instead, I get a little stab in the gut and think, "Urgh, there is too much acid in that cup. This will hurt me to drink." And so I take a few sips because I want them but then have to put the coffee mug down somewhere that I can't smell it because my tummy starts to cramp and complain loudly about its perceived abuse.

I want my coffee! I want it now! I want to throw myself on the floor like a three year old in front of the coffeemaker and beat my fists on the hardwood, like that will somehow make a difference. I would get a brush – maybe like a dryer vent cleaning brush – and stick it down there and clean out the yucky parts that are causing the grief if I thought it would allow me to drink a cup of coffee. I've already tried Alka Seltzer and peppermint tea and ginger. I'm thinking of swallowing a charcoal briquette to see if that will do any good. I don't want IV coffee – I want to sip it, to smell it, to feel the warmth, to enjoy it.

Wake up and smell the Coke Zero. Just doesn't have the same ring to it, does it?

All Wet

So yeah, because I am me, I jumped in the lake the other day with my phone. I put it in a plastic baggie to protect it when we went out on the boat, just like I normally do, except that I used the off brand sandwich bag instead of the Ziploc Bag. So the seal didn't stick. Not that I would normally jump in the lake even if I had used the Freezer Bag. Normally, I would put the plastic bagged phone in the bag with all the towels. But alas, in a fit of unprecedented helpfulness, my children had already brought the towel bag down to the dock, so I stuck the phone in my pocket and then promptly forgot about it. (An aside – the kids never seem to use the towels, as the bag is still crammed with neatly folded towels at the end of every trip, and yet somehow the wet-towel-around-the-house to people ratio stays around three to one.)

Yes, I forgot about my pocketed, bagged phone until I yelled, "Cannonball" and flung my middle aged body off the side of the pontoon boat and then felt something rectangular bang against my leg as I plunged in the water.

I tried drying it out, and I got it to the point where I could make and receive phone calls using the blue tooth thingie in my car, and sometimes I could receive phone calls using just the phone itself. It intermittently worked otherwise. But not mittently enough, so I was forced to go get a new phone. Blah blah, I won't bore you with the transaction, except to say that somehow I was convinced this go round to buy the insurance, despite the fact that the math didn't really seem to work out unless I kill the phone within the next six months or so. Which, I guess, is likely, given my proclivity for, well, for being me.

It's not a huge deal, goodness knows, since for the first thirty or so years of my life I didn't even have a cell phone. Modern society, however, especially modern momming and lawyering, requires that you not go five seconds without responding to a phone call/email/text message, etc., lest someone assume you are either dead in a ditch without the ability to so much as call home and leave a message or that you are deliberately ignoring the sender and making a very personal comment on what you think of their needs. Horsehockey, you may say, and I won't disagree with the editorial comment about the hockeyness of the horses, but I triple dog dare any of you to deny the prickly reality of it.

Like any new electronic purchase, the first three or four hours or so of ownership are devoted to setting the blamed thing up and trying your best not to throw it across the room when it doesn't cooperate. I mean, how am I supposed to remember my Instagram password when the last time I had to remember it was the last time I got a new phone? I can't even remember what email address I used to set it up, since I have about 17 email addresses, all used for various purposes, and all with different POP-3 server codes (whatever that is) if I want to get the emails on my phone.

There's also the games, AKA things to do while wearing a paper gown sitting on a high table for 45 minutes in a doctor's office. Plants vs. Zombies is my favorite phone game. I've killed a lot of zombies in my day, and to be perfectly honest there are times when shooting at cartoon zombies with Pea

Shooters and blowing them up with Potato Mines is better than a glass of wine or prescription medication for taking my mind off of the worries of the day and relaxing me. I'm good at Plants vs. Zombies, better than my kids even, which is saying something for a woman whose high score on Flappy Bird is 1. On my old phone, I unlocked all the bonus rounds and mini games, and had completed nearly all the Achievements. My Zen Garden was robust, and I had coins to spare. Now I have to start from scratch, and that may be the part that makes me the saddest about this whole phone ordeal. After all, all the good pictures I had already uploaded to Facebook.

I'll get over it. The fact that I can do all these things while sitting in my weather-tight air conditioned home I can actually afford, sitting in a comfortable LaZBoy with an over full belly and drinking the non-pathogen-laden beverage of my choice proves that I don't have any real problems.

But STILL. I had all the icons where I wanted them. All my passwords were memorized. Life was good, and Zombies didn't stand a chance.

Ah, who am I kidding. Those Zombies still don't stand a chance.

I Like To Clean

I have a confession to make. This confession will surprise anyone who has seen my house, which looks like a weather system
has just blown through my living room and the Red Cross has
not yet arrived to relieve the disaster. (Not for nothing, but the
weather system – a triple threat involving stuff-tossing wind,
furniture shifting earthquakes, and water/soda/juice down-
pours – has the non-coincidental name of the other people who
happen to live in my house.)

My confession is this: I like to clean. I do. There is something very therapeutic and powerful about creating order out
of chaos. Think about it. Nature doesn't particularly care for
order and right angles. (Don't talk to me about the rhythmic
beauty of fractals and crystals, and how soap bubbles always
join at 120 degree angles – as these patterns of nature do not
support my analogy, I am conveniently ignoring them.) Rivers
don't flow in straight lines. Wild blackberries don't grow in
neat hedgerows. My hair, which is naturally very straight, and
so you'd think it would just hang straight down in a boring
way, doesn't even obey the laws of gravity. Right now, for
example, only an hour out of bed on a lazy Saturday morning,
I am sporting a 'do that is best compared to the Heat Miser's.

I feel like a pioneer when I tackle a big cleaning project.
Like I'm going into unchartered territory with the goal of civi-
lizing a plot of unused land for crops.

In my house, these expeditions can also be archaeological.
For example, yesterday I uncovered a notebook that my kids

used for scribbling and doodling some years ago. Apparently after discovering "Harriet the Spy" in approximately 2009, my son decided to spy on us and take notes. Dad was "huming and washing dishes loudly." My husband then came over to me and said, "want some fried cheese." My son's then opinion was that "fried cheese" "might be cod name." [Sic.] If we kept things neat and organized, I wouldn't have the pleasure of finding these little treasures.

The biggest problem with cleaning, however, is that you start to realize the filth you have been living in. I guess I get accustomed to the level of basic grunge and it just starts to look normal to me. Then I clean the bathroom. And suddenly, the sparkly clean countertop and bathtub makes the grout look dull. So I wipe it with a washcloth and realize from the residue that the texture of the tiles has allowed dust to collect on top of the swells. There goes another twenty minutes of my life. More, if I need to get a Q-Tip to get the dust out of the uneven places in the caulking. Then the newly uncovered white grout between the tiles on the wall highlights the dull grey of the grout between the floor tiles. So there I end up, on hands and knees in the bathroom with an old toothbrush, wedging my head behind cabinets and bending my arm in unnatural angles so that there is no clear line of demarcation anywhere between where I have cleaned and where I just got tired of trying to reach.

I can only do these things when I am in the house by myself, which isn't often, and probably explains why it gets to the level of bad that it does before I do something about it. I recognize how ridiculous these things are and how obsessed I become. I am conscious of my over-sized posterior sticking up in the air as I reach behind the commode to clean out the crack between the porcelain and the floor. No one needs to see me like this. Plus, I like to do this while listening to my 'blocker outers,' which is what I call my MP3 player, because the ear buds block out everything outside my head and allow me to reside entirely in my brain. When I am listening to music like this, deep inside my own head and unaware of any sentient beings not living in my skull, I have a tendency to sing along, loudly, whether or not I know the words. There is not a person in the world whose life is improved by hearing me sing.

Eventually, I finish. I am usually bone tired and a little bit sweaty, and maybe lightheaded from being in close quarters with cleaning fluids without proper ventilation. But it smells clean and looks shiny. There is order and harmony in a little corner of the world, and I made it happen.

There are so few things in this world I can control or even adjust to my liking. It is such a powerful feeling when I can. The feeling doesn't last – eventually – usually shortly -- someone else comes home and splashes water on the mirror or gets toothpaste on the sink and/or leaves a wet towel or dirty laundry on the floor. But for a moment there, the world bends to my will, and I like it that way.

(Im)Patiently Waiting

I think I spent about three-quarters of my waking hours the other day standing behind someone in line trying not to have my head explode. It was tough, and I am now exhausted.

It started out at the gates of Club Fred, aka Pelican Preserve, the 55 or better community (NOT a retirement community) in which my parents live in Ft. Myers, FL. As I am not a resident, and have no interest in plowing through the gate, I have to go through 'security.' As much of a coward as I admit to being, I'm pretty sure I could take any of the guards there if it came down to it, not that I have any interest in doing so, as following rules makes me feel safe and secure. Anyway, there was a car in front of us who was apparently, from the length of time it took and the number of interactions between driver and guard, catching up with all the details of his life with his long lost twin brother that he hasn't seen since second grade. Then it was our turn.

We pulled up to the gate. I know we are on my parents' list of permanent good guys, so there should be no requirement that anyone get in touch with my parents to see if the dangerous looking minivan full of iPods and stuffed animals and bathing suits and tired looking people was going to come in and vandalize the place. We announced our names, and the names of my parents, whom we were visiting. My maiden name, Brudner, is for reasons I never quite understood fairly unpronounceable for most people. People never mispronounce Rita Rudner's name, and routinely handle "Bruckner," but substituting the "ck" for a "d" or removing the frontal "b" throws people for a loop. So we had to repeat the name a few times. I admit this offended me a little bit, as if my parents were famous and worth knowing and how DARE he pretend they were just one of hundreds of people aged 55 or better living on campus. Eventually we were given our pass, along with an extremely friendly but not needed or wanted (my daughter's teeth were floating in the 50 million ounces of root beer she insisted on getting from the RaceTrac 100 miles back and she was rather vocal about her discomfort) explanation of how it was good for six months, and so we should hang on to it, and my parents' street was just down the road and to the right and GOT IT JUST OPEN THE GATE THANKYOUVERYMUCH.

A little while later I went to the grocery store to pick up the ingredients for my world-famous guacamole, since my mother discovered 45 minutes before the actual event that she was actually supposed to bring something in a pot to a pot luck. It doesn't take me long to make guacamole, and the store was just around the corner, so I figured I had plenty of time. I picked out the avocadoes and the other necessary items, and flew to the express line. There were two men in front of me. One had groceries already bagged in his basket, and the other just had a few items in his. The 'regular' lines were long. Two other folks got in line behind me, each with under 15 items, like I had and like they were supposed to.

Turned out the two guys were together, and had bought what had to be 75 items. They wanted to pay for the items with a check. Apparently the concept of a checking account was new to them, because they had to have help in filling out the check.

ID was proffered, and the cashier put the check in the scanning machine. Swishswish. And again. And again. She pushed some buttons on the keyboard of the cash register. Then swish-swish again. Swishswish. Swishswish. More buttons. More swishing. More ID checking. More pointing at checks. Then the calling over of an Assistant Manager who looked like she had just come from her 10th grade history exam to her after-school job. The Assistant Manager typed some things on the keyboard. Then swishswish. Swishswish again. More typing on the keyboard. Swishswish. Swishswish. This took a looooooong time. So much so that my ten year old daughter, who was with me, said, "What is the problem?"

Usually Socratic in my teaching methods, I said to her, "What is the definition of insanity?"

She knew this one. I use it a lot. "Doing the same thing over and over again and expecting a different result."

"Good," I said, praising my daughter for her ability to learn. "That is what is going on." This was right before the actual manager, who did appear old enough to buy beer, came over to do some swishswishing of her own. I finally caught the cashier's eye. "Is there any way you can void them out and deal with them at customer service so the rest of us can get through?"

"Sorry," she said. "We can't save a transaction and move it. We have to void it out."

"That's what I'm saying," I said. "Void it out and re-ring it up at customer service so the rest of us who have been standing in line in the "express" line can get through." I admit it, I used exaggerated, physical air quotes around the word "express" to make my point.

I tried really hard not to roll my eyes when she said, "sorry, we can't," but I don't know how successful I was. I did not jump over the conveyor belt and throttle her, which at that moment was my fondest wish. I did not and would not because such things are illegal, and I wish to set better examples for my impressionable children.

Eventually it occurred to the manager to send the cashier over to the empty lane behind us so those of us wedged in the "express" line could get through. I made it back to my parents' house with all of 96 seconds left to get the guacamole made. I was only a few minutes late. No one had to wait for me or my guacamole.

But if they had, it would have been worth the wait.

I'm Dreaming of A Pink Selectric

I had a dream the other night in which I found a pink IBM Selectric II typewriter in a Goodwill shop run by my grand-mother, who has been deceased since 1989. Analyze that. I dare you.

For some reason, I can't quit thinking about that typewriter. In the dream, my grandmother had told me that anything I found in the shop I could have. The shop was set up in an old house, and there were lots of rooms and nooks and crannies. I was with a man, who I presume was my husband, but didn't look anything like my husband. When I found the typewriter, sitting on an old school desk, I sat down and touched the keys reverently. I'm pretty sure a beam of sunlight came down and illuminated it, and there might have been a heavenly chorus.

Some of it is easily explainable. In my office, we actually do use a typewriter from time to time to fill out pre-printed forms. We have a decent enough typewriter, but all three of us who ever use it are old school typers and we all agree on the superiority of the IBM Selectric as a typewriter. We keep looking for one at garage sales. I'm pretty sure I will never find a pink one. As far as I know the only options were 'black' or 'putty.'

I remember being a little kid and we had one of those ancient typewriters with the arms that would strike the ribbon to imprint the letters on the paper. The arms got crossed if you typed too quickly. Not that I could type all that quickly back then, but sometimes I would just hit random letters because I liked the sound of it so much. At that time, during the Mesozoic Era, there was no such thing as a home computer, and the only way to make things look neat and professional was to type them. I loved the sound of a typewriter. I loved the ding at the end of the line, and the physical act of returning the carriage to the start position for a new line.

Then came the electric typewriter. You no longer had to physically move the machine to the beginning of a line, and there were no more arms, but rather balls or wheels that imprinted on the ribbon. Some could even remember a few key strokes and delete for you so you didn't have to use White Out and blow on it so it would dry more quickly and you could get on with your typing, albeit with a crusty spot where the White Out was.

The IBM Selectric, as far as I'm concerned, was the king of these. The keys had a nice feel to them. The ball was easy to interchange so you could actually *change fonts!* No longer were we stuck with Times New Roman, although to be honest I almost exclusively type in Times New Roman because I like it.

Now, of course, I use a computer to type almost everything. Probably because I wrote several thirty page papers in college and had to retype the entire thing every time I made an edit, I can now type about a hundred words a minute. I am old enough now that most modern 'improvements' irritate me. The slimmer the laptop or keyboard, the less likely the keys are to have any heft to them. You can't always feel the position of the keys. Right now I am typing on an old brontosaurus of a laptop that still runs Windows XP despite the fact that Microsoft no longer supports the 14 year old software and I keep getting warning messages that my computer will self destruct if I don't upgrade. I have within arm's reach a new fancy schmancy convertible laptop with a touch screen, but I use it almost exclusively to play games. I can't bear typing on the wimpy little keyboard. I am forever accidentally typing things and making weird things happen with the heat of my hands.

I think I like typewriters and keyboards whose keys actually 'click' and need a little bit of force to push because I want my words to have some heft and substance to them. It is the same reason that if I am going even further back in time and need to write something on a piece of paper in the random mess of scribbles I call my handwriting, I prefer using a pencil. There's more drag on the paper. More connection between the writing instrument and the words. Virtual keyboards are for texting and quick emails. Facebook comments. Things that don't matter.

The bottom line is this: if you happen to see a pink IBM Selectric II typewriter at a garage sale, let me know. I'll buy it at any price. Even though my grandmother said I could have it for free.

High Score

Although there are many things to recommend the place where I live, "number of things to do" isn't one of them. So when you consider that, and the fact that I memorized all of the patterns in Ms. Pacman decades ago, when "Flashback Games" opened up in Loganville, I was thrilled to pieces.

There's big money in nostalgia. Now that I'm in my 40s, it is my generation that is in charge of most things and fuels the economy. Which means that nostalgia for the 80s fuels a lot of commercial engines. This is why there are legwarmers for sale completely without irony at Claire's, neon nail polish is all the rage, and all the purses are metallic leather with fringe. And also why a place that is filled with vintage video and arcade games from the 80s had a line of people waiting last Sunday for it to open.

You wouldn't really think that the simple graphics would appeal to the younger generation, but somehow they do. I've brought my children – and their friends to this arcade a few times, and I get tired before they do. Which, of course, is the usual way of these things, I mean, me getting tired first. But not of things they don't like: they tolerate the XM radio channel 80s on 8 for only a song or two before they are ready to flip it to SkankRadio or whatever it is that plays Ke$ha songs.

I love this place. It reminds me of the Pizza Machine arcade on Long Beach Road in Oceanside, NY. I spent hours there in the 1980s, and dozens upon dozens of quarters figuring out when exactly Donkey Kong was going to throw those barrels and when to pick up the hammer.

Aside from the nostalgia, I still really like playing these games. I like simple games with one joystick and one, maybe two buttons, if any. I like uncomplicated rules. I don't want to think too much or have to do anything that requires any form of physical coordination. I like Ms. Pacman. I like Centipede. I like Dig Dug. I like Space Invaders.

We went last weekend and stayed almost three hours. They have a great system there, where you pay one price and get a wristband, and then can just play whatever you want as long as you want so you don't need to use quarters. I admit I found myself getting a little crazy. We got there when it opened, and apparently they reset the high scores every day. So I could go machine to machine and get the high score. Only sometimes I'd come back to a machine and found out someone – probably one of the three balding guys who were the only other grownups playing – had beaten my high score. So I had to try again. I turned into a competitive crazy person. I had to beat RLS, whoever he was, and no hand cramp or sweaty palm or repetitive stress disorder or full bladder was going to stop me.

I OWNED those games. I could BEAT those games. Every time I succeeded I had to drag my son and his friend over to witness my glory. At first they thought it was cool. Then they thought it was funny. Then they thought I had just lost it.

It got a little ridiculous.

Galaga was my undoing. I played a lot of Galaga in my day, even beyond the 80s, when I was in law school and there was a Galaga machine in the Laundromat where I did my laundry. I would carefully figure out how many quarters I needed to get my clothes mostly dry and use the rest to play Galaga, leaving my law books lonely and unread on the table. There are two Galaga machines at Flashback Games, and for a brief, shining moment I had the high score on both machines.

And then some guy came by. I never saw his face, because he was leaning into the machine. His hair was thinning, and had a few gray streaks, but his arms and legs sticking out from his garden variety polo shirt and khaki shorts didn't seem to have any age spots or sagging skin. In other words, he was about my age. He was intense. He played a long time. And when he walked away, there was a score I couldn't beat. I tried, Lord knows I tried, but I couldn't do it. And then, when I looked at the Centipede machine, I had been knocked down to numbers three, four, seven and ten. This was horrible! I played again. And again. And again. I supplanted my own third place score a few times, but couldn't get higher than that. I slapped my hand down on the console every time I foolishly ran into the spider thingie. And when I was in final reach of RLS's score, the little guy that drops down pooping out mushrooms slammed me, and I was done. I yelled. It was a guttural sound, no words, just the vocal version of frustration. My son was playing some Kickboxing game behind me and he turned around. "What's wrong?"

"Nothing. I just can't beat this dude's score."

He patted my head like you might do a small child or a puppy or a lunatic, and turned around to go back to playing his own game.

Right about then I decided it was time to go.

But I'll be back. I MUST save the world from alien invasion.

A Year Of Living Medically

Amateur Eyeball Surgery

It was a lovely day for eyeball surgery. The sky was overcast. Very little sunlight penetrated through the wet air to make a glare or make my pupils contract involuntarily. My husband, Mike, drove me to the surgery center. At the ripe old age of 43 I found myself with a cataract that made everything on the left look like it was swimming in Vaseline. Whenever a bright light shone towards my left, as with oncoming traffic at night, I was treated to a blinding white glare. Surgery had to happen. I wasn't nervous. I admit, I was really looking forward to the opportunity to lie still with an IV drip of tranquilizers. Yes, that is what my life has become – I look forward to eyeball surgery because of the Verised.

The first worrisome question of the day was what to wear. Since I was going to a surgical center and not a hospital, I didn't know if I'd be required to wear a fashionable backless hospital gown, or just allowed to wear what I wore in. So should I dress like I have a full time job and some sense of pride, or do I just say to heck with it and wear the yoga pants and a t-shirt? The yoga pants won. Yum. Snuggly.

After signing a whole bunch of paperwork promising not to sue anyone if my eyeball accidentally popped out and rolled down the hallway, I was placed on a hospital type bed and covered with a warm blanket. A kind nurse asked me which eye we were operating on, and I pointed to my left and, where I pointed, she initialed my forehead with a purple Sharpie so that there would be No Mistakes. The eye doctor and the anesthesiologist both did the same. As I write this, four days later, it looks like I got a prison tattoo of a bottle of moonshine on my forehead.

Then came the IV drip. The lovely, lovely IV drip. An oxygen tube was placed in my nose, which I thought was overkill until I realized there was a very real possibility that with these powerful tranquilizers, breathing might just be too much effort to bother with. So, on pure oxygen and powerful drugs, and under a warmed blanket, the nurse asked me what might be the stupidest in the history of stupid questions: Are you comfortable?

It is weird being awake for surgery, and hearing the doctor talking to the nurses. I don't remember everything because, frankly, the day dreams in lalaland were much more interesting than the names of the different scalpels and tweezers. I do remember that my previously implanted phakic lens was difficult to get out and so a different kind of tweezers needed to be used, and the incision had to be enlarged. This resulted in 'leakage', which in my loopy state I pictured as a gelatinous goo resembling partially cooked egg whites spilling out of my eyeball, and so some stitches had to be put in. Yeah. Eyeball stitches. I've got 'em.

At some point it all ended, and the IV was disconnected (sad face) and I went home and slept for the rest of the day and following night while dressed like a pirate. (No, the eye patch did not come with a parrot.) I woke up the next morning sick to my stomach, my usual feeling the day after anesthesia, but

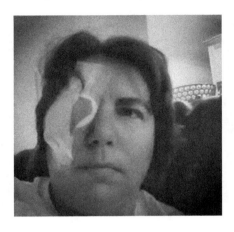

managed to hold it all together until most of the way to my follow up appointment, when I found it necessary to make my loyal driver pull over on the side of the road so I could lose what little breakfast I ate. Which leads to an etiquette question. What exactly is the protocol when making an emergency stop to vomit in someone's yard? Does one send flowers? Leave a note? See if there is an outdoor hose for surreptitious use? We chose the 'cut and run' option. Sorry, random folks. I hope the grass grows greener in a patch of your yard.

The surgery was a success, and every day I can see better. I only had to rock the indoor shades for two days, and now my eye merely looks like I had a rough night. The tape holding the patch on, however, is some kind of industrial magic tape which should be used to replace duct tape for all your fixin' needs, as no matter what I do I can't get all the glue off my head. I blew dry my hair yesterday morning and the hair stuck to my forehead in a permanent windswept pattern.

Oh well. At least it covers up my prison tattoo.

Cough Cough

My daughter came home from school with a cough, and passed it to me while my defenses were down as I recovered from eyeball surgery. (Sorry, but it is just really fun to type and say 'eyeball surgery' and every time I do I hear giggles in my head.) I got this cough last week, on Wednesdayish, and it is a Tuesday as I write this, and I am no better, if not worse. I don't know what it is. I finished my course of antibiotics. I'm dutifully using the inhaler that makes me shake like I'm jonesing for some crack, and taking the steroids that made a friend of mine say today, "You're mean when you're sick." Now I'm waiting on the results of my chest x-ray. I'm hoping for something curable but Victorian like Consumption of Pleurisy rather than something mundane and modern like bronchitis or pneumonia.

One thing is sure: when this is over, I am going to have some serious rock hard abs. My entire abdomen aches from the kind of exertion the teeny tiny muscles in there aren't used to. (I don't have a six pack. I don't have a beer belly or a pony keg. I'm thinking maybe I have a little juice box of a muscle – or maybe a Capri Sun pouch, since it doesn't have regular corners – surrounded in a great big protective layer of cushioning so it can't leak.) And you women who have had children out there…you know what happens when you cough really hard and your pelvic muscles are enlisted in expelling the bacterial invaders….

I'm not a very good sick person. Nope. Not at all. I don't take very good care of myself. Of course, I chalk this up to actually having to take care of myself instead of just lying in bed like a four year old, having someone bigger and more nurturing and loving and competent reading me stories, and bringing me popsicles and glasses of juice and my medicine at the right time with little cups of water, and steaming bowls of homemade chicken soup. Nope, I made my own chicken soup, shopped for the ingredients and peeled and chopped the vegetables while certain other male adult members of my family who shall remain nameless sat in the La-Z-Boy and watched TV shows about cars we can't afford.

I've tried to stay away from work, but it hasn't worked well for me. I actually went to Court on Monday, since I had no choice. You can't just fail to show up at Court without getting permission from On High, which I couldn't get on a Sunday night when the situation became inevitable. My representation of my client consisted largely of my waiving my hand in his general direction and mumbling something like, "I represent that guy, I think, or maybe that guy, or maybe that lady over there, my cold medicine makes it difficult to tell, and I'm too sick to actually cross examine a witness. May I please be excused before I infect everyone in the building?" (The answer was "Yes.") I went to work today, and got all my emails and phone calls returned, but was chased out by my co-workers who didn't want pieces of my spleen being coughed up on them at regular intervals. I had to give someone a check, but I thoughtfully sprayed it (and my hand) with Lysol before handing it to her. It was only sort of a joke.

So what do I do now? I've gotten a lot of writing done, posted a lot of inane things on Facebook, and watched enough

TV to make me remember why I don't usually watch a lot of TV. So now what? I've done a bunch of reading, and even started knitting a scarf, but those are precision viewing things, and my eye still has stitches in it and isn't fully recovered.

Speaking of which, I'm told it isn't medically possible to cough violently enough to pop my eyeball stitches (almost as fun to type and write as eyeball surgery) and spew eyeball goo across the room, but I'm not convinced. Also, can I really say it is the steroids that are making me mean when I'm not saying anything I wouldn't have *thought* under other circumstances?

In conclusion, I want a cup of hot tea. Brought to me on a tray. With honey in the tea. And lemon. And maybe a teensy tiny shot of bourbon, for strictly medicinal purposes. And I don't want to have to ask for it.

P.S. It turned out to be pneumonia. To which my father said, "Good. They can cure that."

The Pickleball Chronicles

I went to the Jewish homeland (south Florida) Christmas week so I could eat Chinese food and go to the movies with my parents and allow them to coo over and spoil my children rotten. My parents live in a resort-style 55 or better community my father, Fred, refers to lovingly as "Club Fred." One of the newest amenities is a set of pickleball courts. It replaced the basketball court that once stood in its place that I never once saw an actual resident using.

Apparently, no one north of Orlando (and 50% of those south of Orlando) knows what pickleball is, so I will explain. In a nutshell, pickleball is tennis for little kids and older folks. But, apparently, not for middle aged folks with coordination issues. The court looks like a miniature tennis court. I'm told it is the same size as a badminton court, but telling me something is the size of a badminton court is as useful to me as telling me exactly what is wrong with my car would be. Or maybe less, since at least if I knew what was wrong with my car I could have some idea if I was being ripped off by a mechanic. The rules for serving and scoring in pickleball are more or less like those of ping pong. The net is low, maybe waist high. The rackets look like oversized ping pong paddles, and you play with relatively slow moving hard softball sized wiffle balls.

We were playing doubles. Me and my son on one side, my mother and daughter on the other. My father and uncle were watching us and making fun of our inability to volley. My daughter hit the ball in my general direction. It was short and low, so I leaned down and ran forwards in an attempt to get it. I missed the ball, but had a lot of forward and downward momentum. I couldn't figure out how to stop without falling on my face. The court is small, maybe only three or four running strides across, and I really hadn't planned well. I kept running, trying to slow myself down without a spectacular America's Funniest Videos worthy crash. I figured worst case scenario was that the net would catch me. And so, still bent over from my ill-conceived notion that I might actually hit the ball, I slammed into the net.

I don't have a personal recollection of what happened in the next few seconds, but my son does. He can't tell the story without laughing, and then apologizing for laughing, but it seems accurate enough, so I will use his version. I bounced off the net, and the sudden shift in momentum from forwards and down to backwards and up made my feet slide out from under me. I landed hard on my rear and, using another example of my poor physical instincts, I reached out my left (non-paddle) hand to break the fall. What made my brain think that landing on my palm would be more comfortable than landing on my well-padded backside I will never know.

I do remember my mother shouting, "What are you? An idiot?"

The next thing I knew the feelings of pure embarrassment and excruciating pain were competing for space in my brain.

I am no stranger to injuring myself in humiliating ways in public places, and I know that if I keep calm, don't overreact, and practice my deep breathing for a minute the pain usually subsides and I have a funny story to tell later. So I sat on the pickleball court and focused on slowly filling my lungs and waited for the throbbing to stop.

It didn't. My family surrounded me and fussed over me. Eventually, I managed to stand up and get myself into my parents' golf court, golf carts being the main source of transportation at Club Fred. Someone thrust a small towel filled with ice at me, and I put it on my wrist, directing my father to take my place in the game while I rested. My uncle, who was himself hobbling on a cane due to his recent hip replacement surgery, told me stories of other people injuring themselves in embarrassing sports related ways to cheer me up. It did work a bit, as laughing at the misfortunes and injuries of others is a Great American Pastime. Schadenfreude is as American as freedom fries, no? This explains the popularity of TV shows like AFV and Fear Factor and ice hockey games.

After about five minutes, I peeked under the ice. My hand was swelling rapidly, and there was an odd lump near where my thumb meets my wrist. "I think I'd better go to the emergency room," I said. My uncle peeked over and agreed and announced the good news to my parents.

So let us review: I was able to injure myself playing a sport (pickleball) designed for people with limited mobility but, apparently, maximum coordination. Now that I've had some time to reflect I will just have to focus on the fact that if no athletic gifts have shown up in my physical makeup in 43 years, they probably aren't going to ever make an appearance. My ability to cook, talk, schedule an appointment, and handle three conversations at once will have to do.

But I'm realizing, looking over what I have just written, that I left out an important detail in the story. What I failed to describe, however, is what I was wearing, which is essential to picturing the whole fiasco accurately in your mind's eye. You might picture me wearing something passably athletic, like elastic waisted shorts and a t-shirt advertising some charity event I went to 15 years ago, since I was in public playing an athletic game. You'd be wrong. No, although I was wearing high quality running shoes and athletic socks, the rest of my outfit consisted of an old bathing suit bought years ago in an "It's December and Please, Please Get Those Bathing Suits Off Our Hands" sale. On top of the bathing suit was a schmatta. For those of you unfamiliar with the term, schmatta is one of those incredibly useful but difficult to define Yiddish words. It literally means something like "rag" but is generally used to describe a raglike garment. Shapeless dresses, an old moth eaten sweater, your favorite sweatpants with the hole in the knee: these are all schmattas. Mine was a formless bathing suit cover-up, gauzy and semi-see through, and bedecked with sequins. So you can imagine that I looked rather stunning. Not stunning as in, "Wow, that woman is so beautiful I can do nothing but stand in my tracks and stare." Stunning as in, "It is stunning that a grown woman would allow herself to be seen out of doors wearing that get up."

Now that you can picture me, let us reset the scene: my swollen and misshapen wrist made a holiday (December 22nd) trip to the ER inevitable. My dad drove me back to his house in the golf cart so my husband could take me to the ER in a real, street-legal car. Eventually, after some stress-related scream-ing at each other by the adults I am related to by blood and/or marriage, I was loaded into the car and we headed off to the nearest hospital, which was about fifteen minutes away from my parents' house.

We found the hospital easily enough, due to directions from my Dad and the G.P.S. The entrance to the Emergency Room itself was not so easy to find. We ended up going into the hospital complex by a weird entrance probably made for ser-vice vehicles only. There were signs pointing towards the ER, but they seemed to send us down ridiculous winding switch-back paths through the parking lot, mapped out by the same guys who make the waiting line for rides in amusement parks. Naturally, every six feet or so was what felt like a speed moun-tain instead of a speed bump.

The speed bumps made me yelp, because they jostled my wrist. Every time I yelped, my poor husband thought it was a comment on the smoothness of his driving, which it sort of was. This made him bark. Between the yelping and the bark-ing, any observers probably thought we were heading to the insane asylum, or the veterinary hospital. At this point I would have settled for the pound so long as they had heavy duty pain killers designed for Great Danes.

Eventually, after as much driving in the parking lot as in the roadway, we got to the Lee Memorial Hospital. They called me back before the sign-in paperwork was finished and I had to get my husband to finish it up. He attempted to put up his regular fight about how I am better at paperwork than he is and it should be my job, but I then showed him my arm and he shut up and continued.

The triage nurse sat me in a room and took my vitals and typed them into a computer. I noticed he kept typing the word 'deformity.' I will grant you the word was accurately descriptive, but it felt the same as if he typed the similarly accurately descriptive, 'middle aged woman wearing bizarre getup and enough extra weight to feed the Donner party for a week.'

Eventually they sat me in a chair in the middle of the hallway. I assumed this was because the rooms were full, but it might also be because it made it easier for the hospital staff to say something like, 'check out the crazy deformed woman on hallway 3' to each other than 'find an excuse to go into exam room 2 to check out the whacko in there.'

After some failed experiments with pulling and grease, it was determined that my wedding and engagement ring would have to be cut off. By this time, my husband had finished the sign in paperwork and had found his way to my hallway just as the guy was putting together the hospital grade Dremel tool. I guess Mike's brain protected itself by worrying about an inanimate object instead of his injured wife, and he insisted on placing a piece of paper under my hand in order to catch any platinum dust that might fall during the cutting procedure. He then got into a heated debate with the Dremel tool operator about the proper way to cut a ring. This resulted in his leaving the emergency room under questionable circumstances. I'm not mad at him, by the way. I'm actually sort of flattered in a twisted way that seeing me injured made him act as crazy as I looked.

Then it was off to the x-ray room. The x-ray tech wanted me to lay my arm down on the plate in different positions. I could not move or twist my arm in the ways she wanted me to. As a result, I kept my arm stiff and moved and twisted my body so that my arm could be in the place she wanted it to be. This weirdo yoga, combined with the fact that I was not technically wearing any pants, would have made for an entertaining video which thankfully does not exist. (To my knowledge, it doesn't exist, that is. There's probably a security video somewhere that the nurses watch during their lunch breaks to make themselves laugh.)

By the time I got back to my hallway suite, the x-ray had already been emailed over and I was given the precise medical diagnosis of "oof, you really did a number on yourself." I looked at the screen. Normally, when I look at x-rays it is similar to when I look at early term sonograms. I believe you when you tell me what it shows, but I can't see it for myself. This, however, was obvious. The top of my radius was cracked and shifted over and little spiky bones were coming out of the sides.

My arm was splinted. I was allowed to choose the color of the splint, and I chose red in honor of it being so close to Christmas, with the idea that I could make it look festive by using white duct tape to approximate a candy cane. Yeah, I was that stoned. I was sent home then, in a Vicodin induced haze with instructions to see an orthopedic doctor ASAP.

Just when we were getting ready to leave the hospital, my husband, Mike, announced that when he looked inside the specimen cup used for storing the engagement and wedding rings cut off my finger, he noticed one of the side stones on my engagement ring was missing. I was settling into the good part of a Vicodin haze. So, I wasn't too upset about the missing quarter carat diamond. I had bigger worries and stronger, drug-induced things to care about beyond an inanimate object, as sentimental as it may be. I went back to where I was sitting and searched for the diamond. I was helped by the original triage nurse and the ring cutter. We couldn't find it, and the general consensus of the hospital staff was that it had fallen out when I fell on the pickleball court.

By the time we got back to my parents' house, my Mom had already called her friend Alan, the retired groinocologist (as my

father would say) to get recommendations for orthopedists. He had friends. I was to call his friends as soon as I woke up in the morning, which I did. Despite the holiday and last minute nature of my requests, I was able to get an appointment for late morning on December 24th.

I was very tired by the time I had the appointment. Sleeping was no small task. I finally figured out that a giant, round, vaguely creepy stuffed turtle named Chubsy, originally purchased as a pillow/cushion to protect me from the ground up razor blades apparently used as stuffing on the second bus used by the 5th grade safety patrol trip to Washington DC last May was the best arm prop. (You can find that whole story and enjoy some additional schadenfreude in my first book, Mismatched Shoes and Upside Down Pizza.) Chubsy came with us to Florida because he is an excellent car pillow. After the arm disaster, I took Chubsy with me wherever I went. Still do. To the movies, restaurants, doctors' appointments – Chubsy is my faithful companion. Pair Chubsy with my winter schmatta, a poncho with a hood that I knitted myself while watching hours and hours of continuing education video tapes, plus the hair I can't blowdry, and pants only of the elastic waist variety, since I don't have enough use of my left hand to navigate a button or zipper, and you might find yourself thinking, "Wow! She looks clean for an obviously untreated schizophrenic just rescued from her cardboard box/home under the railroad tracks."

But I'm getting ahead of myself. On the day of Christmas Eve I went to the one orthopedist who didn't take off for Christmas. (This is not the first emergency medical situation I have ever been in on December 24th, but that's another story for another day.} X-rays were taken again, and yet another X-ray tech said something like, "Holy Moley you really messed yourself up – come look at this!" I went back into an exam room, where a P.A. came in and told me they were going to set my arm, but not to worry, they would numb it first. By numb it, he meant stab a needle the size of my pinky finger into my already broken wrist over and over until he got tired of me yelling. I thought he meant there were drugs in the needle, but it felt more like he was trying to sever the nerve. Maybe both things were true.

Then the doctor came in. He explained that he likes doing things 'old school' by manually setting the bones and holding them in place with a cast going from first knuckle to mid bicep. And so began the setting. I was told to lie down and press my right side against the wall. The PA and the doctor grabbed my arm and someone – the doctor? – began pulling and squeezing my arm in the way that you might pull and squeeze a tube of toothpaste to get the last molecules of minty freshness out because you are too lazy to go rumbling in the closet for a new tube. If the numbing, stabby needles worked at all, you'll have a hard time convincing me. I screamed like I was auditioning for the part of "expendable sorority girl #2" in a horror movie. When the squeezing and yelling stopped, I discovered that I had remained pressed against the wall, but my legs were stiff and pointing towards the ceiling. Not sure what reflex in my brain thought that would help. Probably the same one that made me land on my wrist instead of my heavily cushioned booty. I found it in me to laugh at my legs. "You know," the doctor said, "This is much easier if you pass out."

"I'm trying!" I yelled back as he started one more round of squeezing. Eventually, it ended, and as a consolation prize I was allowed to choose the color of my cast. Knowing I already had tickets to the Chik-Fil-A Bowl on New Year's Eve, I decided to accessorize for the occasion and get a Duke Blue cast. Go Devils! Never let pain or stress get in the way of supporting a deserving team.

We were able to find the diamond that fell out of my ring at the ER when my husband went back to the hospital to get my X-Rays prior to meeting with the orthopedist. The diamond was wedged against the wall behind a trash can near the chair he had been sitting in at the hospital waiting room. Never one

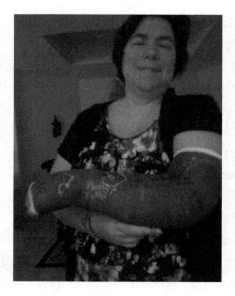

to leave well enough alone, he opened the specimen cup containing the ring to inspect my poor cut wedding rings while he was waiting, and the diamond must have fallen out then. I do admire his dedication to the task. I believe him when he said everyone was looking at him as he crawled around on his hands and knees with a flashlight in the middle of a public waiting room.

Anyway, my arm had just been set and put into a Big Blue Cast that weighed approximately 75 pounds. I found myself unable to complete the simplest of tasks. My dislike of the woozy feeling I get from narcotics was outweighed by my dislike of the throbbing, stabbing feeling I got without them (and by my dislike of the accompanying toddler-like whining sound I made.) Therefore, between the cast and my being pretty well stoned, I was fairly useless and needed to be babied. I hate this, by the way. I pride myself on being strong and independent and I, well, wasn't.

At first I washed my hair in the kitchen sink using the squirty thingie with help from kids who believed they'd hit the lottery because they were allowed to squirt Mommy's head with water. I used washcloths to clean the parts of me I could reach with my right hand. Eventually I felt too disgusting for these stopgap measures and decided I would take a bath. My husband and mother jockeyed for the "Who Takes Care of Lori Best" trophy. As a result my mother's guest bathroom was full of grown people arguing about the best way to secure a Hefty bag around my arm in a reliably waterproof way. Eventually, my husband wisely realized he was arguing with a momma bear protecting her injured cub and left the bathroom.

It was then, four or five days after the Great Pickleball Fiasco, that I saw in the mirror, spanning my entire décolletage and continuing across my right arm, a purple line: the bruise mark, apparently, from where I slammed into the pickleball net. Nope, being bathed by my mother at the ripe old age of 43 wasn't humiliating enough.

I am proud to report that I survived it, despite some touch and go moments.

Somehow, my family made it back to our home on December 26th. I made an appointment with an orthopedist here, who cut off the Big Blue Cast and replaced it with a Big Brown Splint, which only weighs 20 pounds, a vast improvement. The plan as it stands now is to put a metal plate and six screws in my arm to hold the mess together and prevent the fragmented bone from collapsing on itself. Along with my bionic wrist, I will be receiving a doctor's note to carry around in my wallet to use whenever I go through a metal detector.

Because one medical disaster per family is not enough if you are a Duff, the day before my surgery, my husband went to the hospital to get four cortisone injections in his lower spine so he could walk without hunching over or limping. He drove there, but he was being semi-sedated so I had to drive him home. I forewent my pain meds so I wouldn't have to drive impaired. I looked a mess – I took the ever-present Chubsy and kept warm with my schmatta/poncho. My hair was matted on one side where I had napped on it. I entertained myself by playing dumb computer games in the waiting room. Eventually the nurse came out and told me to bring the car around. I pointed to my broken arm and indicated I couldn't move so quickly.

Somehow, with one arm and no pain meds to soften the blow I was expected to carry Chubsy, my purse, my computer, and my husband's jacket to the car with me. I wondered how I was going to pull it off and decided that I should pull out my keys now to avoid having everything fall and go splattering across the parking lot. I looked in my purse. I checked my pockets. Aaaaaand, of course I couldn't find them. I had a very specific memory of putting them in my purse, so I knew they should be there. Unloading my purse and looking for my keys without another hand to hold the thing up so it wouldn't tump over was proving difficult, so I embarrassed myself further by asking the nice couple I'd been sitting near for close to an hour to help me. While they were unloading the random contents of my purse, the wheelchair guy stuck his head in the room and gave me a "why haven't you gotten the car yet?" face.

I said, "I can't find my keys."

I heard my husband mumble groggily from the hallway, "I might have them." And so he did. Why he took them out of my purse is yet to be determined. So, the nice stranger people reloaded my purse. I thanked them, dumped Chubsy and Mike's jacket on Mike's lap, and went to bring the car around.

As I was pulling the car around, my phone rang, and it was the folks from the hospital I was going to calling to give final details. I have a built in Bluetooth in my car, so while the folks at Clearview Hospital were loading my husband into the car, the lady from the other hospital was blaring through the speakers to schedule my surgery for the next day. This level of pitifulness made me laugh such a way that I feared that the nice young men with the clean white coats would shoot tranquilizer darts at me to make it stop.

And then I sneezed. I am over 40, have had babies the regular way, and was hysterically laughing.

I'll give you one guess what happened next.

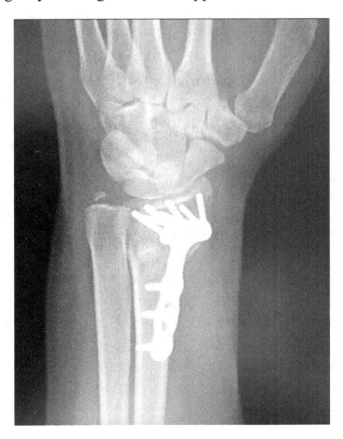

Gold Stars For Me

I had my second session of physical therapy today resulting from the Great Pickleball Incident. My friend Sheri, who works at the Y in Lawrenceville, gleefully told me a few weeks ago that they are now offering Pickleball at the Y if you want to try it yourself.

Anyhoo, at the first PT session, the therapist measured all the ways my fingers and wrist could (and could not) bend. This morning, I came in fairly certain that not much had changed in the past four days. After a 'who's on first' type conversation that went something like this: "It's your left wrist, right?" "Right." "Your right wrist?" "No, my left wrist." "Left?" "Right." I got to stick my hand in this odd contraption that blows hot air and ground up corn husks all over my hand and wrist while I make figure eight motions. I love this thing. It is warm and toasty and comfortable, so much so that even though I don't and will never smoke, I kinda want a cigarette afterwards. The only problem with it is that afterwards for about an hour I am picking out what feels like grits from under my fingernails.

Then came the measuring. To my happy surprise, I had improved quite a bit, and the therapist complimented me on the obvious 'homework' I had done throughout the week.

This made me unreasonably happy. I am a 43 year old woman who has one and a half successful careers at the moment, two children who just might be the most perfect beings on the planet, and I get my biggest thrill of the day from being told by someone I am paying for services that I did well.

This is typical of me. Most people dread going to the dentist. Not me. Nope. I brush and floss like a good girl, cannot bear the feeling of the fuzzy plaque that builds up around my gums, and haven't had a cavity in so long that I couldn't tell you when it was. Definitely not since my kids were born, and my eldest is 12. Every time I go to the dentist, I get a metaphorical pat on the head for actually flossing. I get a surge of pride when told I have no cavities. I have an urge to call my mother and tell her so she can praise me, too. Curiously, I get almost more pride from these things than I get from victories in the Courtroom, but not as much as when my children do anything even remotely clever.

I don't know why this is. I like pleasing authority figures. Even though I know better now, I still have this desire to believe that all authority figures are in positions of authority because they are knowledgeable and good at their craft (as opposed to being well connected or in the right place at the right time.) Therefore, they are (theoretically) better than me at whatever they are doing because otherwise I wouldn't need them to do it. I know this is true with both the physical therapist/hand specialist and my dentist. I have no idea how to do either one of those things.

So, and this should surprise no one who has ever met me, what we've established here is my nerd credentials. I like being the teacher's pet. If you are teaching me how to do something, or evaluating my work product, I like to be told I've done a good job. Don't we all? I might just be a little more extreme than other people. Or maybe more honest. I say things from time to time like, "Aren't you proud of me? I remembered to bring my files home from the office."

If you see me in the near future, don't be afraid to scratch me behind the ears and give me a treat like the good dog that I am. I will reward you by wagging my tail.

Medical Mike

My husband is suffering from a disease he calls "Old Man Syndrome." He just turned 60 and, as he sees it, his parts are starting to wear out. He hasn't been in any bad car accidents, or had any on-the-job injuries, or any major slips and falls. (That's my department.) The latest thing to go out has been his back.

I shouldn't really say "the latest thing." His back troubles have been going on for some time. Four years ago he was told he was going to have to have surgery, and it is only just now that he is getting it. He had a fusion of a disc in his lower back – L3 to L4, I believe, for those who pay attention to such things. This means (I think – I am not fluent in medicalese) they took away the bone that was falling apart, and replaced it with some metal mesh and a bone graft taken from his hip and screwed it to another bone for stability. I know. Ew. Ew and Ow.

The lead up to the surgery was typical Duff Family Frustrating. My husband, being a combination of his own unique self and a stereotypical guy (not to be confused with a man – for further explanation of this phenomenon see Dave Barry's Guide to Guys) was able to give me exactly no information before the surgery beyond, "I am having lower back surgery on June 30th. Dr. Price is the surgeon." That's it. He couldn't say what kind of surgery, nor specifically where in his back, what the recovery would be like, nor even what hospital it would be in. In fact, the best we could do on our own was narrow it down to four different hospitals in three counties.

The week before the surgery, Mike decided to take one last hurrah of a fun trip before being laid up for a while, and went to St. Augustine with some of his oldest and dearest friends. He still had no idea where or specifically when (morning, noon, or night) the surgery would be, or when he had to be where for pre-op. I finally gave up, and drove over to the surgeon's office. They knew me there, because when I shattered my wrist last December due to my inability to stay upright while attempting to play a low impact sport, and had to have a bionic wrist put in, I used the same orthopedic group. I walked up to the front desk and announced, "Allegedly, my husband is having back surgery with Dr. Price on Monday. He doesn't know which hospital, what time, or when his pre-op is. I'd like to know." I knew from experience that they have a little form that asks you if they can give your information to anyone else, and I knew that Mike would have given me permission, so I wasn't worried about HIPPA.

After disappearing in the back for a moment, the wonderful, helpful lady out front gave me more information about my husband's back surgery in two sentences than my husband had given me in several months. We were going to be at St. Mary's in the morning, and his pre-op was on Thursday. I called him and informed him that he might want to come back from Florida on Wednesday.

And so came the surgery. I was unfortunately unable to attend the pre-op due to that day job thing I have to pay bills with, and was required to rely on him for information. He was either going to stay in the hospital one day, or two days, but whether that meant there were potentially one to three overnights, could not be said, at least by him. He might go home that day. He might have to stay a few nights. He might be able to walk around afterwards, or he might be completely immobile for a few weeks.

I usually pride myself on my ability to prepare for contingencies, but I admit I completely dropped the ball this go round. I'm going to blame Mike for his lack of specific information going in, but that's not really fair. Knowing I didn't know, I should have been prepared. I guess I thought I would have more mobility. I was prepared to wait during the surgery. I brought a book, my Kindle in case I finished my book, two different computers (one that is a good workhorse for writing and one that is a great toy to play games on), a notebook and pencil, and a hank of yarn and two knitting needles. I was Good to Go.

The surgical waiting room, however, was a complete disaster. It was relatively small and was nearly standing room only, as people kept coming into the room and no one seemed to be leaving. One family brought what seemed to be 25 relatives with them to grandpa's surgery, which doubled as a family reunion. There were two other couples, stereotypically nice, friendly southern folks, who had an incredibly polite (high volume) conversation for two hours about church camp, prior surgeries, and diabetes. Another very large gentleman wearing short athletic shorts propped himself on the sofa across from the chair he was sitting in, leaned back at an angle so steep I thought he might have trouble getting back up. He splayed his legs in a most unladylike fashion, and proceeded to try to sell computers from his cell phone in something that could not by any definition be called an "indoor voice." There were a smattering of other folks who kept to themselves, and a very kind lady who sat next to me working Sudoku puzzles and not bothering a soul except once an hour or so asking me to watch her stuff so she could use the restroom. There was so much conflicting chatter, along with the yaddayaddayadda of the ubiquitous television set turned to a channel no one was watching, that the only thing I could concentrate well enough to do was to text my friends and write "To Do" lists in my notebook.

Finally, the surgeon came out to tell me all had gone well. All I could think was, "I can leave the room! I can leave the room!" (Oh yeah, and I was happy my husband's surgery went well.)

I headed to Mike's room where I waited for him to be wheeled in. And then I waited. And then I waited some more. It was a good hour and a half before he joined the land of the conscious sufficiently to be taken out of the recovery room.

When he came into the room, he was a peculiar combination of still-sorta-under-anasthesia: feisty, confused, irrational, and in pain. It was somewhere at this point when I realized how truly unprepared I was for this ordeal. I was as delusional about the process as I was about what life would be like with a newborn baby in the house. Back in pregnant, ignorant bliss, I imagined sleeping, sweet, snuggly babies, resting comfortably on my chest while I read good books. That happened for maybe five minutes a day. Then I got what everyone else gets, which is a crying, demanding, sleep-depriving, eating, pooping machine that doesn't even so much as smile back at you for six weeks.

That same thing is, more or less, what I had in a husband post-surgery. He slept ten minutes of every twenty, woke up, demanded food or other assistance, and then went back to sleep for exactly enough time for me not to be able to do anything productive, including get my own self some sleep or rest. Like a fool, I had brought some work with me and books to read, imagining my poor, morphined husband peacefully sleeping while I Got Things Done. I did not, however, bring a tooth-brush, a bar of soap, a change of underwear, or even a particularly comfortable pair of pants. I don't know what I was initially thinking. Probably that he'd be so doped up that he wouldn't notice if I went home for the night to sleep in my own bed and shower in my own shower. I am a fool.

No, the first night, after he finally got drugged enough to be comfortable, and I felt like it was safe leaving him for a few minutes, I asked someone in scrubs what time the cafeteria closed. I was told 6pm. As it was about 8pm when I asked the question, it was a most unhelpful answer. Even if it weren't, it is still a ridiculous time for a restaurant to close. Unless, of course, you are in south Florida where the majority of the population eats at 4:30. We weren't. I was told there were vending machines on the first floor (I was on the 6th) and so I wandered down to see what I could find.

As vending machines go, they were good ones. They had yogurts and microwave burritos and questionable looking sandwiches. In the end, I chose a Cup O'Noodles, because I knew I could find hot water somewhere (but not a microwave) and a small can of pineapple chunks. Oh yeah, and a pack of mint gum to make up for the lack of oral hygiene.

I went back up to the room to eat my gourmet meal and find out if my pitiful husband needed help rolling over. (He did.) After what passed for dinner, I went about making my bed. It was a chair, covered in rather hard, non-breathable vinyl (for easy clean up for goodness knows what kind of bodily fluids and whatever else has been spilled, dropped, oozed, or splashed on it over the years). Once I got down on the floor and figured out how to unlock the wheels, I pulled it away from the wall, only almost knocking over the IV pole once, so that it had room to recline. I had been given two sheets, a stiff blanket, and two crunchy pillows. I didn't want to make the 'bed' until I had reclined it, so I got in it and found myself scooting all across the room as I pushed back because I had forgotten to re-lock the wheels. Then when I finally got it back, I was the picture of grace trying to figure out how to get out of it without having it fold back up or slip back on the slick floor.

And so, fully dressed, I settled in for the night. Sort of. Anything resembling rest in a hospital is purely coincidental. Nurses and techs and orderlies were in and out all night, administering medications and taking vital signs. All of which does not count the tremendous ordeal it was when Mike wanted to roll over or change positions, which required my assistance and strength and getting ookily close to some frightening looking wound dressings.

About 6:30 am, the surgeon came back in to check on Mike. He was showered and peppy looking, and I sort of wanted to punch him in the face for it. He pronounced Mike "as good as can be expected" and informed him that, like it or not, he'd be getting out of bed that day.

Several restless hours later, the physical therapist came by. She informed Mike that he was going to get out of bed and take a little walk. He was skeptical. I sat back for the show.

Think about it: if you had to keep your back perfectly straight and had virtually no core strength, not to mention being stoned on a narcotic cocktail that would drop a full grown gorilla, getting out of bed would be quite the accomplishment. And so, wearing that most flattering and revealing of garments, the Hospital Gown, and wearing socks with no-slip treads, he learned how to bring up his knees, log roll over, scootch his feet and legs off the side of the bed, use his arms to lift his unbending torso, and sort of slither off the bed without bending forwards. I was proud of him for only moaning and groaning a little.

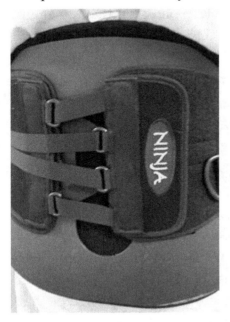

He was given a walker, and shuffled a circuit around the tiny room, with me moving IV poles and blood pressure monitors and tables and chairs and all manner of other floor hazards out of the way like the guy with the broom in Olympic Curling. While he was standing, his back brace was put on and adjusted. I was pleased beyond rationality to see that embroidered on the side of this huge black thing that covered most of his torso was the brand name "Ninja." He might be as far from a ninja as he could get at that moment, but I loved the inspiration. Yes. This is the back brace that ninjas use. It is a stealthy back brace. The people who wear it are avengers of evil and lethal, if morally righteous, weapons.

I put my 'bed' back into the upright and locked position, and he sat in it for about an hour as per instructions from the physical therapist. Thirty minutes of that hour was me arranging and rearranging pillows behind his back and head and under his knees until he was tolerably comfortable. After that, the physical therapy session declared a success, he reversed the process by sitting on the side of the bed, kind of tumping over, and logrolling back onto his back. I was as proud as I was the day my son took his first steps.

Naturally, after that, he fell asleep and didn't get up again, even though he was told he should get out of bed from time to time and take a few steps. I didn't push it. Later that day, our good friends brought our children by to see their father. He mostly slept, and they mostly ignored him by playing on their iPods and begging me for money to go to the cafeteria and get ice cream. I had them bring me a change of clothes and a toothbrush, which they did, even if of all the shorts I had on my shelf they chose the shorts that gave me the biggest wedgie. I was able to get a bar of soap from the gift shop, as well as a book of crossword puzzles. Of course, the gift shop didn't have any pencils, and only one pen, which was oversized, and said something like "World's Greatest Nurse" on it. After enough whining on my part, the sweet clerk gave me a chewed up, half used up pencil from the cup near the cash register. I was very grateful.

On day two, the physical therapist came back. She made him get up out of bed without the use of the walker (since it might scoot out from under him and he would fall) for which he still refers to her as "That Physical Therapist [insert unflattering expletive here]." From there, he trudged into the hallway to get in line behind a number of other Hospital Gown clad and walker toting patients so he could learn how to walk up stairs without killing himself (or me.) Since he did not, in fact, kill himself (or me) (or the physical therapist), we were pronounced ready to go home and given our discharge papers. The discharge papers said, among other things, that he should not be in a car for more than a half hour. This was a problem, since we lived well more than a half hour away from the hospital. I chose to pretend I didn't actually read that line.

Having been tagged and released into the wild, we made it home, and Mike made it into bed without incident. Our bed, which is very high off the floor, proved to be much easier to get in and out of than the hospital bed, which encouraged him to completely overdo the up and down thing.

Around ten o'clock that night, I realized that I felt hot and sweaty. Due to my age, and the fact that I am hot natured to begin with, this is a familiar feeling, but it felt humid as well, and I asked if anyone else was hot. They were. I looked at the thermostat, and saw that despite the AC being set on 73, it was 80 degrees in the house. Fan-freaking-tastic. Well, at least we had several ceiling fans, that is.

Normally, when our air conditioning goes out, which happens once every year or so, I tell my husband, Mike, and he does whatever he does, and then boom, the air conditioning is working again. Given the fact that he was at this point stoned out of his gourd (legally) and unable to walk, much less navigate the long steep stairs into the basement or bend and twist and do whatever physical labor was required to fix the air conditioning, it did not occur to me to ask him to do anything about the problem. So I did what I always do when something I can't solve on my own happens: I posted something on Facebook and then went to bed.

I woke up relatively early, with a heat and humidity induced migraine which felt like someone had stabbed an ice pick into the brow ridge of my left eye. I made my way into the bathroom, took my medication, and then sat on my knees waiting for it to kick in with my head on a pillow in the chair beside my bed, the only position I could find which wouldn't result in an explosion of brain matter. I am happy to report that my brain did not, in fact, explode, but my stomach did, an unfortunately common side effect of migraine pain. The advantage of the hurling is that while horribly unpleasant, it does generally signal the dying breath of a migraine.

Quite a healthy pair we were, my husband and I.

It is notable that this was now July 3, 2014 which is not only the day before a holiday, but my husband's 60th birthday. There's something of significance in that, but I haven't quite worked it out.

With the pain in my head subsiding, I went to check my computer about lunchtime. I was rewarded with a private message from a friend who said that her husband was an HVAC guy, and would be happy to head over, only it was her husband's birthday, too, and he had celebrated with a couple of beers at lunch, in case that was a problem. I informed her that I wasn't aware that men were capable of fixing anything without a beer or two in their systems, and as long as he could get here safely, it didn't make me no nevermind.

I was proud of myself. A relative crisis came up that is normally not in my realm of control, and I got it handled. I went to my semi-conscious husband and informed him that he need not worry his sutured body and fuzzy mind about this problem, as I had a Guy who could come over and fix it.

I'm going to blame this next part on the lingering effects of anesthesia. I refuse to believe that any rational part of a man I would marry would do what he did.

He reared up, yelled, "I'm still the man in this house!" and proceeded to get out of bed and try to get dressed. Somehow he managed, and shuffled over to the basement stairs. My newly-grown-taller-than-me son and I tried our best to block his way but, alas, even sedated and crippled, my husband is bigger, stronger, and quite a bit more forceful than either of us.

He did make it down the stairs, and over to the blower in the basement. I convinced him to give instructions to our son rather than do things himself, which worked until my son got tired of being yelled at and wandered upstairs. The AC guy came, driven by my friend, and went around the side of the house to take the cover off the AC unit. I convinced Mike to quit working on the blower and meet the AC guy. He went out the basement door, and began naming air conditioning parts as they were exposed in order to prove that he was, in fact, a fully functional guy who could handle these things on his own and didn't need help, despite whatever his emasculating wife was posting on Facebook.

Long story short, the AC got fixed, and Mike made it back in bed (eventually) after walking around the house and coming in the front door and then walking down the basement stairs again and back up them.

I guess I'm a mean person for feeling vindicated that it was about two days before my husband could move again without crying out in pain. He blames it on the physical therapist who made him get out of bed without using the walker. Me? I'm pretty sure it was the basement stairs and attempt at home repair. But what do I know?

We had plans to spend the weekend of the Fourth of July at the our house on Lake Oconee, and since Mike could lay around in bed and sleep and do very little anywhere, there didn't seem to be any reason why the rest of us shouldn't spend a summer weekend at the lake.

Superficially, Mike seemed to be doing better. That is unless you actually listened to the things he was saying. He had some fairly entertaining prescription drug induced hallucinations. At one point, I was told rather emphatically that "Dr. Bruce needs the tape recorder." When asked for clarification, he said, "You know, the VCR tapes."

The next day, after a fairly lengthy conversation in which I insisted that it was, in fact, Saturday, which seemed like a difficult concept to grasp, he insisted that I was a half hour late picking up our son. "Where do you think he is?" I asked, knowing full well that he was in the next room playing Call of Duty 4. "I dropped him off," he said. "At the place." He couldn't get any more specific. It took some convincing that poor Mikey hadn't dropped anyone off or even driven a car in over a week.

And, just when you thought it couldn't get any more pitiful, it came time for the Changing of the Bandages. I'm good at a lot of things, but I also recognize my limitations, and blood and ooky stuff are not what I'm good at. There was gauze on his back and hip, held by large sheets of clear tape. The ones on his back seemed ok, but the one on his hip was frightful. There was some angry looking skinless red that could be seen under the clear tape, and there were some raised patches that looked like blobs of Nutella. Or alien parasites. I wanted to haul him to the ER, but he decided, without being able to see what I was looking at, that he didn't need to go. There's no reasoning with a guy under these circumstances.

So I did the next best thing. I ran next door and got our neighbor, a retired gynecologist. As a lawyer, it generally irritates me when people expect me to be an expert in a field I don't practice in: something I only knew a little about to pass a law school exam over twenty years ago. So I knew that Beverly's specialty had nothing to do with what I was dealing with. All I really wanted her to do was to tell me if I had to go to the ER or not.

She flew into action, though. Apparently gynecological surgery and back surgery are a whole lot different on the inside, but not so much on the outside. Booboos are booboos. Sutures and dressings are sutures and dressings. On her instruction, we found some rubber gloves over the washing machine, a bunch of Q-Tips, some peroxide, a bottle of ancient Bactine, a cup of water, and a roll of paper towels. It was my unfortunate job to hold a paper towel beneath the affected area to catch the peroxide and other disgusting drippings so they wouldn't get on the chair or the floor. Blurgh. Blech. Even just remembering it my stomach is seizing up and throwing punches at my brain for the recall. I am NOT GOOD AT THESE THINGS. There is a very good reason WHY I didn't go to medical school.

Eventually, we got the whole thing re-bandaged and hidden from my view. I rewarded Beverly with a bottle of wine and an autographed copy of my first book and a fifteen minute spew of thankyouthankyouthankyous.

Like everything awful, excepting Death and Taxes, this, too, shall pass. As I write this, more than a week after the last described episode, he can get up and down and roll over all by himself, and as far as I know he hasn't attempted to fix any more appliances. (I did find evidence that he climbed a stepladder to do goodness-knows-what with the curtains in our bedroom, but I'm conveniently choosing to ignore that......)

Put What? in Where?

Now that I am middle aged and overweight enough to be able to carve a middling-sized yellow lab out of the extra weight hanging off my body, I find that I have begun to snore. I don't know how much of this has to do with the aging process, or the gaining-weight process, or if that is unrelated and it has more to do with the fact that I live in metropolitan Atlanta and this is spring.

There are few things more beautiful than spring in the deep south. Everything blooms. Even the weeds are pretty. Things are lush and colorful, and you see everything through a yellow green haze. The crayon closest to that color is called "spring green," not because it matches the tender young leaves emerging from hibernation, but rather the pollen that covers everything. This pollen is visible. You can scoop it off your car in handfuls. It fills your eyes, throat, and nose. There are days when I swear it blocks out the sun.

The human body was not designed to withstand this kind of assault. If you look at a grain of pollen under a microscope, it looks like some variation of a ball with sharp pokey things sticking out at all angles. If you wear contact lenses, you might as well just rake your cornea with a fork for all the comfort you will experience. The immune system's response to this invading, prickly army is to have all the tissues in your head swell to repel the invaders, and when that doesn't work, to catch them in as much sticky fluid as your poor little overwrought mucus glands can produce so they don't filter into your brain and cloud your thinking. I think your head suffers the most because it has the most holes in it exposed to the elements.

If you didn't have allergies before you came to Atlanta in April, you will soon enough.

The only kinds of medications that give me any relief make me stupid tired. The kind of stupid tired where you are talking on your phone while trying to get out the door and announce to the person you are talking to that you can't leave the house yet because you can't find your phone. So those meds are out. But many days my head feels so full of funk that if it were possible to install a little spigot on my cheek or right above my eye to release the pressure I would do it no matter how ridiculous I looked. So I looked for alternative remedies.

The concept of the Neti Pot made perfect sense to me, even if the concept skeeved me out in equal measures. For those of you unfamiliar with what a Neti Pot is, it looks like an Aladdin's lamp kind of thing. You fill it with purified salt water and, while tilting your head, pour it in one nostril so that it fills up your sinus cavities, gives them a quick rinse, and comes flooding out the other nostril. Definitely not something I would do recreationally, but, well, desperate times call for desperate measures. After taking an informal poll on Facebook and finding that a surprising number of my friends had done this (I, apparently, am the only one who discusses these things publicly) and had Very Strong Opinions about methods, brands, and solutions, I went to Walgreen's and bought myself one.

There were several choices, one of which was battery powered and promised "pulse irrigation." I did not choose

 that one for what I assume are obvious reasons. I went with what looked like the simplest. I took it home, and boiled some water in the microwave, so as not to get any tap-water borne brain eating amoebas that close to my innards. I let the water cool to approximately 98.6 degrees, and mixed it in my little plastic pot with a packet of finely ground salt and whatever other minerals the good folks at Walgreen's put in there. Following the directions, and imitating the embarrassed-looking model in the picture, I looked down into the drain, shoved the thing up my right nostril, tilted my head to the left, and poured.

I was warned by the directions to breathe only through my mouth during this procedure. This seemed a rather obvious piece of advice, as a) it would be counter-intuitive to breathe through your nose while pouring salt water into it and b) I was so nervous about the thought of having that water in the nose feeling for the rest of the night or perhaps drowning myself accidentally that I didn't breathe at all. I felt the warm water flood my skull and then begin to pour out of the other side. When the water stopped flowing, I blew my nose like I was supposed to, and then repeated the procedure on the other side.

I have to say it worked. I did not get that water in the nose feeling, despite the potful of water in my nose. My head felt empty and clear of pollutants for the first time in recent memory. The only bad side effect was that when I stooped down to tie my shoe an hour or so later, a lingering dollop of water came splashing out. A little salt water on my shoe was a small price to pay for comfort, though, and I recommend this to anyone with nostrils big enough to fit the spout in. Just don't ask me to demonstrate it for you.

Honest Doctors

My friend Carrie, the world-renowned psychologist I referred to a few chapters back when I talked about the Cheetos I served in a Tiffany Bowl, brought up yet another excellent point the other day. Her son had to have some impressions made of his teeth. Anyone who has ever had impressions made of their teeth knows that the process involves putty-goo filled trays that are only just small enough that you don't choke on them, and chomping down on the putty-goo filled trays for what feels like 72 million years while the putty-goo sets. You spend the 72 million years they are not-quite-choking you trying to figure out what to do with your tongue, besides trying not to swallow it; suppressing your gag reflex; trying not to drown in your own saliva; and generally wishing you could pass out to make the time go faster. There is nothing about this that is fun. While it is not necessarily painful, neither is waterboarding or sleep deprivation or listening to Miley Cyrus at high decibels, all of which are considered torture according to the Geneva Convention.

In other words, it is awful. A necessary awful, perhaps, but awful nonetheless. So Carrie's point was this: why did the person putting the putty-goo trays in her son's mouth feel the need to reassure her son, "This won't be so bad" and then, after removal say, "See? That wasn't so bad." It was bad. It was a horrible thing to have gone through, and by telling Carrie's son it wasn't going to be bad and then that it wasn't even though it was, the nurse completely diminished her son's accomplishment: that is, suffering through it without a panic attack or tantrum.

So, on behalf of Carrie's son, and on behalf of all of us who have ever been told, "You'll just feel a little pinch," before being stabbed with what feels like a rusty, frozen ice pick, I hereby propose legislation which would require doctors, dentists and other medical professionals to let you know what you are in for. In other words, don't lie. In the words of the brilliant jurist Judge Judy, don't pee on my leg and tell me it's raining.

I know as well as you do that being honest isn't going to make it hurt any less or be any less torturous. When I brought this idea up to some of my friends, they thought it was horrible because it would make them panic if they knew what was coming. My retort is this: if you are over 10 years old you've been there and done that a few times and you know you are in for it anyway. An acknowledgment of what we're in for by the people doing it to us will allow us to feel pride in our accomplishments. For example: let's say you have to get a filling. As it is now, the dentist will numb your gum and inevitably say, "you'll just feel a little sting" or something like that. Then a needle the size of a drinking straw is shoved through your gum and it stays there poking up against the root of your tooth and your nerves while the Novocain gets injected. Then you get your tooth drilled, and while it doesn't hurt, exactly, you have to keep your mouth wide open for a very long uncomfortable time, and listen to that horrible grinding noise, occasionally get a piece of tooth flung up at your face, and sometimes smell something vaguely burning. When it is done, you are given a pat on the head, told to floss more, and sent on your way.

Wouldn't the following scenario be better? You sit in the chair. The dentist gets the turkey baster sized needle out and says something like, "Ok, this is really going to hurt like crazy, but I swear to you it will hurt less than if I drill your tooth without it." Then, while all the drilling is going on, instead of talking with the assistants about what to have for lunch or the schedule for the afternoon, the dentist would keep up the mantra, "Sorrysorrysorrysorrysorry, I promise I am doing my best to make this go as quickly as I can." When it is over, the dentist would say, "Phew! Thank you so much for not biting me or punching me in the head when I accidentally hit the nerve. That was some great self-control you just displayed. Now, the side of your face is going to be numb for the next couple of hours, so don't drink anything or it will dribble down your chin and make you look like even more of an idiot than the slackjaw does. When it wears off, you are going to feel like Mike Tyson punched you in the side of the head, so here's a fistful of Motrin and a voodoo doll with my likeness on it for you to stab with pins."

Then you could leave feeling like you accomplished something. Like you braved something painful and scary and uncomfortable, and came out of it stronger for having done it. Because the truth is, you did.

I Chose To Reproduce For A Reason. Even If I Can't Remember The Reason Right This Minute

Mall of Torture

I just might be the bravest person you know. Oh sure, there are police officers and fire fighters and soldiers out there who selflessly put their lives on the line every day for perfect strangers, but I -- I alone -- took three tweenage girls to the Mall of Georgia. Yes, I was alone with these girls for approximately 8 hours. Yes, I know you think this is the sort of thing people are generally sentenced to as opposed to doing voluntarily, but I am selfless and benevolent like that. Plus, I am bat-poop crazy.

To mitigate the circumstances, these were exceptionally good girls. They are all straight A students who originally bonded over the Percy Jackson and Heroes of Olympus series of books. They refer to each other by their 'goddess' names: Athena, Artemis, and Minerva. They are all polite and

119

considerate and loud and giggly and squealy. And so cute it makes my heart hurt.

This trip was in lieu of a birthday party for my daughter. The original deal was that we would go to Universal Studios in Orlando (specifically Harry Potter World, or whatever it is called) during fall break instead of having a birthday party in January, her real birthday month. We did go to Universal, and it was fun, but my son's birthday fell in the middle of our trip. I'm all about getting whatever free birthday stuff can be gotten whenever and wherever it can be gotten, so every time we sat down to eat for the day before, of, and after I announced loudly to whomever might possibly be in charge of giving away birthday favors that it was his birthday. This made my daughter, um, Minerva, mad as only a preteen girl can be because we were there for HER birthday, and why wasn't anyone making a fuss about HER???

So, after three months of a ginormous chip on her shoulder, I caved, and took her and her besties on a little adventure in shopping.

Let me say right here that although there are some forms of shopping I like OK, I cannot bear the Mall of Georgia. Most likely, all the things I dislike about it are the same things my daughter does like about it. There are swirling masses of humanity, all starting and stopping without warning and going in unpredictable directions and all carrying packages they occasionally whap into you by accident. Most of the stores play loud, horrible pop music. There are lots of stores selling identical merchandise that no one needs but everyone wants. Plus, I was in charge of two little girls who were lent to me by their parents for the evening and they were both shorter than my daughter, and therefore easy to lose in sea of grownups. If I had a nickel for each time I said, "Girls! Stay together!" I probably could have bought anything in the mall, up to and including those very tempting calf massage chairs at The Sharper Image.

For reasons unclear to me, the girls insisted on going to the La-Z-Boy store, though I'm sure none of them were interested in buying furniture, even if it did have a remote control footrest. They ran in all giggly and would all cram themselves into one chair, make a flurry of noise, and then find another chair to cram themselves in. A poor saleswoman kept trying to talk to me, and I pretended to be interested in a coffee table, which I actually was fantasy-interested in, so as to justify our loud presence in the otherwise peaceful and grown-up store. I barked at the girls at one point to quit running, at which point they all spontaneously, as if choreographed, began walking up and down in the aisles like they worked for Monty Python's Ministry of Silly Walks.

They then went to the room in Charming Charlie's for kids called Charlie Girl. For those women out there who have never been to Charming Charlie's, let me tell you what you are missing out on: acres of color coordinated costume jewelry and accessories at reasonable prices. Seriously girly, sparkly heaven. The girls debated and looked, and eventually bought matching purses. The purses are really stinking adorable, and it makes me sad that I am probably thirty or more years too old to get away with carrying one just like it. The purse is pink rubber and has ears and a face on it. At first I thought it was a pig because of the piggy pink color, but the nose is all wrong.

Minerva said it looked like a panda mixed with a flamingo, and so calls it her "flamingear" (pronounced fluh-MIN- gair.)

Then we went to Barnes and Noble's, where they flew up the escalator to find their beloved Percy Jackson books. I was afraid they would leave behind their Charming Charlie bags in which they had stuffed their old, non-pink vinyl purses, so I offered to hold them. Since I was still wearing a hard, post-surgical contraption on my left arm because I shattered my wrist playing Pickleball, I threaded the handles of the bag over my right wrist. I went to call my son to find out the actual name of a book he wanted, and realized that I couldn't get into my purse with my broken wrist to get the phone, so I had to put the CC bags down. Only I couldn't. I couldn't shake them off my wrist, and I didn't have enough strength in the fingers sticking out from the splint to pull them off. So I was forced to say to the saleswoman, "I have an embarrassing favor to ask. Can you pull these bags off my wrist?" I knew the girls were ok while this was going on because I could hear the giggling. I think everyone could hear the giggling. I did not hush them, because as far as I am concerned, pure, innocent laughter is the best music out there, certainly better than the electronic, auto-tuned, vapid, semi-crude mess blaring from the speakers everywhere else.

The evening wore on, including an entire hour of Justice, home of everything sparkly, animal printed, and rainbowed. (These are not three separate things. I meant the 'and.' You can find anything you want there with all three qualities.) We wandered in a few more stores, ate food court chicken for dinner, and eventually they suckered me in to capping off the evening with a movie, Frozen, which I have to say in all seriousness is probably the best Disney movie ever made.

I was proud of the girls all through the afternoon, evening, and night, despite their occasional obliviousness to their surroundings and blocking doorways, hallways, and escalator entrances. They wouldn't buy anything unless it could be bought in triplicate, and kept passing money back and forth to make sure that they all had enough to get the job done. Then my daughter fretted that if they all wore their shirts (frugally purchased from the clearance rack at Justice) and purses and 'water bracelets' to school at the same time they would make their other friends feel left out.

Those girls. They really are goddesses.

We All Fall Down

More than once before I have spoken of the archery prowess of my offspring, which contrasts nicely with my inability to aim at and actually hit anything smaller than the Georgia Dome. Last year my son made it to the State Tournament as an individual. This year, his whole team is going. This year, too, my daughter has picked up the sport, and really took to it. (Phew. If she hadn't, I can only imagine what tears and frustration there would have been what with the overachieving brother and whatnot.)

My daughter's regional tournament was in Ft. Valley, GA. If you don't know where Ft. Valley, GA is, don't worry about it. I can't see much reason to go there except for regional archery tournaments. It is about 2 hours and change from our house, and we had to be there at 10:45 on a Saturday morning. There was a huge caravan going from the school that was meeting up at 7:30am. As that was Not An Option for people like us, we chose to go down the night before to stay in a hotel in Warner Robbins. The hotel had an allegedly heated pool. The way our lives go, these little outings are what pass for Duff Family vacations. My kids go nuts over the do-it-yourself waffle irons in the breakfast area. As far as they are concerned, it is worth the price of the hotel room and the hassle of packing up just so they can swim in a bathtub sized hotel pool with frigid water and have a waffle which they will only eat half of.

I am proud to say that the Sharon Elementary School Archery Team won first place in the tournament, and my daughter was the top scoring fourth grader (including the boys!) therefore qualifying both on her team and as an individual for the state tournament in beautiful, sunny Perry, GA in April. (Motto: we're only barely south of the gnat line!) Each team member received a genuine clear plastic medal commemorating their victory. The team was given a trophy for display in the school's trophy case. Except that the trophy was approximately the size of an apple slice. It was a gold plastic archer, no bigger than two inches high. Kudos to the Coaches, who not only gave up their Saturday to go to Ft. Valley with no pay, but who also cannibalized an old high school trophy and glued the teeny award on top so that it could actually be seen in the display case without a magnifying glass.

While I am in no way shape or form diminishing the accomplishments of my daughter and her teammates or the other athletes who were competing, I must say this: the highlight of the tournament had nothing to do with archery.

Let me set the stage for you. Archery tournaments are a lot like golf tournaments. They are very quiet. There is a lot of concentration and focus going on, and the atmosphere, while not silent, is appropriately hushed. No one cheers or yells. There is more muttering under the breath "comeoncomeoncomeonfocus... takeyourtimedon'trush..." than cheers or jeers. The loudest noises are the thwackthwackthwack of the arrows hitting the target and the occasional heartbreaking clatter when the arrow hits the wall or the floor. This particular tournament was in an old middle school gymnasium, with hardwood floors and cinderblock. There were no bleachers that were not in the potential path of an arrow, and so rows of metal folding chairs had been set up for the spectators. We managed to get front row seats directly behind where my daughter was shooting.

For those of you who have either met my husband or read more than three of my essays, you will know that one of the more difficult things my husband has to do in his life is either be silent or sit still. Archery tournaments require him to do both, and he is more or less as restless as your average 4 year old being told to sit still and be quiet during reading time in PreK. So at some point he went to stand up. He had a Family Handyman magazine rolled up in his back pocket for reasons unclear to anyone. The magazine caught on the back part of the chair and began to lift the chair as he stood. When he realized the chair was lifting, he quickly tried to sit back down, only it didn't land back down on all four legs, and when he put his six foot self back down in the seat, the whole thing tipped over in a clangy, echoey way that might have registered on the Richter Scale and dumped him on to the floor.

I could see right away that he was not injured in any medical-intervention-is-needed kind of way, and so I began to laugh. And laugh. And laugh some more. I was trying to be quiet, and so my laughter came streaming out as tears in my eyes. (Mad props to Kimberly Phillips who had the presence of mind to snap a picture of me contorted with laughter while my husband rolled on the ground trying to maintain some semblance of dignity.) The tournament officials and team coaches immediately came over and asked if he was ok, which was more than his wife could muster, I'm ashamed to admit. I'm pretty sure someone asked him to sign a waiver saying he wouldn't sue.

I don't know, I was laughing too hard to register any further facts. I still laugh out loud just thinking about it.

Thankfully, the archers were scoring, not shooting at the time, or I'd imagine they would have had to redo the round. That would have been serious do-over material, though I'm fairly certain there is no "grown man falling out of a metal folding chair" provision in the rule book. It didn't ruffle my daughter at all. She rolled her eyes and soldiered on to her eventual victory. My son laughed hard, more at my hysteria than his father's misfortune. Being Duffs, they're used to this kind of thing. Daddy fell off a chair. Big whoop. It doesn't even ping their radar.

What Does A Gaggle of Girls Say?

I'm playing hooky from work today. I deserve it, I think. In addition to a very long work week which started out with an all day, hyper-dramatic trial, I was one of only two grownups who spent the entire weekend with a troop of Girl Scouts. Yup. Me, another brave Mom (June), eight girls, and a 48 hour slumber party.

It was as non-primitive as you can get and still call it camping, as it occurred in the yard of my house at Lake Oconee. Still, there was no wi-fi or television, we prohibited the use of iPods, and they slept all piled together in one large tent. For these girls, that is downright cave-dwelling. So what if the potties were clean and flushable, and there was a real shower and a real coffee maker and an endless supply of clean dry towels, due to the endless running of the washing machine and dryer? We cooked over a grill (mostly) and spent all day out of doors and ate our collective weight in s'mores.

On the one hand, it was a fabulous thing to watch. Without the influence of boys or men, the girls were free to be themselves without preening and learn independence. Without screen time, they interacted and explored and played in a most old fashioned way. They spent about an hour throwing the anchor off the boat and hauling it up. Why that was fun for them, I will never know, but they were lining up for a turn playing "anchor girl." The youngest girl (my daughter) was in fourth grade and ten years old; the eldest was in seventh and almost thirteen. June and I figured they were old enough that our job was merely supervision. They set up and took down their own tents, built several campfires, and cleaned up after themselves. More impressively, as far as I could tell, they got along the entire time.

There is a downside to a gaggle of girls getting along, however, and that is the constant high pitched "yatatayatatay-atatayatatayatata" that increases in volume as time wears on. They're excited, they're shouting with joy, they're talking over each other, and they are scaring off the wildlife and attracting domesticated dogs. (Seriously – one random dog, who we ultimately named "Bella" because she was annoying us, much like Bella in Twilight does, spent virtually the entire weekend with us wagging her tail, getting petted, and trying to eat our hot dogs. Everyone thought she was cute and friendly up until the point where she got in the tent and peed on one girl's Pillow Pet. We packed her into the car and drove her home a few times, but she always managed to come back with an incredibly hopeful look on her little mutty face.)

But back to the noise. Everything, it seems, is awfully noisy. The constant barrage of sound often feels like I'm caught in a hailstorm of glass shards, there are so many things banging off my skull trying to get in. Right now I am still at the lake, having managed to pawn off my daughter to another Mom to bring home so I could have a few moments of peace. All I can hear is the low tuned wind chimes we got as a housewarming present, the occasional slap of the water against the pontoons of the boat, and about 12 different birdcalls, none of which I can identify beyond "that tweety one" or "the one that sounds like a catcall" or "that screechy one I wish would quit." I haven't turned on the radio or watched a movie or even used my vocal chords in more than 12 hours. The Sounds of Silence. I love it. I never get it.

My house is usually noisy. The dishwasher is running. The washing machine and dryer are spinning. Someone always has the television set on. Someone is practicing the saxophone or oboe or recorder or piano. Someone is listening to the radio. Someone is playing a video game with a bleepybloopy soundtrack. Someone is always talking. Someone is always singing or humming or whistling. Usually all at once. Any one of these things, in and of itself, would be ok, but the combination is an aural assault that the older I get the less I can tolerate. I've tried instituting a "one source of noise in one room at a time" rule, but I haven't been terribly successful, as even my husband won't comply. If you want to talk, turn off the TV. If you want to watch TV, don't noodle around on the piano. My brain is easily scrambled and confused.

I guess I'm alone in this, since the world seems dead set on increasing the amount of input we get at any given moment. You can't even watch the weather without three different scroll lines below giving you information you can't possibly process. I can't shop for anything without a store having 'background' music so loud I have to shout to be heard. Seriously – what does crappy auto-tuned electronic pop music have to do with my choice of blenders? Why does anyone think it will make me want to buy more stuff? It makes me want to high tail it out of the store and shop online as quickly as I can.

I picture my head blowing up like a balloon with all the input. Like all these different bits of information and sounds coming in my ears have mass and are filling up my brain faster than I can mentally digest them. I'm afraid that one day we will all overload, and there will be an explosion. When the shrapnel settles, there will be a lot of headless bodies standing next to clothing racks and holding price tags.

I guess that's not the worst thing that could happen – with no head, there is no way anyone could turn me into a zombie when the time comes. Ah yes. There's always a silver lining if you look for it.

Mother of the Year

So, as everyone in the United States is aware of due to the plethora of commercials telling you what to buy for your mother, spammy emails doing the same, and the sappy Facebook posts about how awesome mothers are as a general rule, this past Sunday was Mother's Day.

Under many definitions of the word, I am a Mother. I have felt justified in celebrating Mother's Day on my own behalf (or rather, allowing others to celebrate me) since 2001 when my son wasn't born yet but was still old enough to kick me in the kidneys from time to time. My own Mother is still alive and worthy of celebration, and I know how lucky I am to have her around to give me guilt trips and aggravate me on a regular basis.

I don't know any Mothers who don't feel guilty on a pretty regular basis. We are all aware of the millions of things we shouldn't have said out loud, the times we lost our temper, our questionable decision making abilities, and our complete inability to vacuum our already clean carpets with a smile on our faces while wearing sensible pumps, a shirtwaist dress, and heels. I don't know about you, but I have a pretty lengthy tally of the things I'm sure my children will be discussing with a therapist for hundreds of dollars an hour sometime in the 2030s.

There are Moms out there who manage to do all kinds of things I am incapable of doing. I'm sorry, but as yucky as school lunch might be it only costs $1.75 that I can prepay in the beginning of the year, and it doesn't require me to have things like non-moldy bread in the house and get up with more than 30 seconds to spare before we have to leave the house RIGHT NOW OR WE'RE GOING TO BE LATE. I only manage to see two out of three notes my children bring home from school (usually written by parents who are more together than I am) asking me to please bring a cut flower from my yard on Monday so we can give the teacher a bouquet for whatever bouquet-giving recognition day it is today. A) If you want a cut flower from my yard it is going to be a dandelion; B) I didn't see the note until two days after I was supposed to bring the flower in; and C) even if I had known I was supposed to bring the blamed thing in I 1) didn't have time to get it cut and appropriately wrapped so it wouldn't die or get crushed on the way to school; 2) probably wouldn't have remembered even if I had the time; and 3) would much rather have just slipped the class Mom, or some other more together Mom a twenty at open house and just told them I was relying on them to pick up my slack.

The problem I have with all this is that despite my inability to do all (or any) of the mommy-like things I know other Moms are doing and feel inadequate for not doing, I really don't think I'm a slacker Mom. Heck --- I am President of the School Council, for crying out loud. I have done career day for seven straight years. I am generally not late to school band concerts and plays, and only miss awards ceremonies if I am more than 600 miles away. (I was in New York for my 20th High School Reunion – what do you want from me?) I tell my kids I love them every day, and haven't throttled either one of them, despite the occasional great temptation. So why do I feel like I'm falling on the job?

I'm going to say that Pinterest and Women's Magazines (the forerunner of Pinterest) have a lot to do with it. Pinterest, for those of you who don't know, is a kind of virtual bulletin board you have, where you can 'pin' ideas for arts and crafts, decorating, recipes, or whatever, and where you can look at what other people have 'pinned.' Overachiever Moms 'pin' stuff like the Thanksgiving cupcakes they made using an Oreo and candy corn as the tail of the turkey. Each of these articles or pins will start with something like, "These were so easy and didn't hardly take any time at all!!!" Oh yeah? Well, you can take your 'hardly any time at all' and put it….ahem ahem, excuse me. This is a book for all ages and I sometimes pretend to be a lady.

Maybe I'm not as organized as some other Moms, or maybe I'm not as willing to sacrifice precious and scarce sleeping hours or alone time in the potty, but frankly I think if I actually show up somewhere relatively on time while wearing two shoes and with my clothing right-side out, I think I've accomplished something and deserve praise. I choose to think of it as teaching my children independence and problem solving skills rather than my complete inability to do for them as much as I'd like. I've already exceeded my Mother's first-day-of-school-breakfast-standard, anyway. She promised to get up early and make us breakfast one year. She did in fact get up early, put an unopened box of Raisin Bran on the table and went back to bed. On the first day of school this year I actually got up early enough to make non-instant grits. Besides, the proof is in the pudding, right? My children are amazing: they are smart and funny and responsible (usually); kindhearted and talented, and downright good looking to boot.

So yeah. Maybe I am a pretty good Mom.

Who Wears Short Shorts?

Shopping for summer clothes for my son was pretty easy. For one thing, as a guy, he will wear anything relatively clean and everything matches blue and khaki and camo, the only real colors his clothes come in. For another, all the boys clothes are a variation on a standard acceptable theme, and haven't really changed since I was in high school back when Jon Bon Jovi was the New Kid on the Block – Bermuda shorts, basic t-shirts, polo shorts for dress up wear, and baggy bathing suits that go down to his knees. Nothing remarkable about any of it.

Shopping for summer clothes for my daughter, on the other hand, made me want to invest in whatever companies still make chastity belts. Or maybe cotton farms, because obviously there is a shortage of cotton and there is such high demand that they don't have enough available to make an entire pair of shorts to sell. I am thankful that my daughter, when left to her own devices, will generally make modest choices. As a result, my arguments were not with her, but rather with the manufacturers of booty shorts made for ten year olds, or the buyers for the stores that chose to stock them exclusively.

I mean, come on. I know I'm in my mid-forties and had the good fortune to grow up in an era when oversized clothing was the norm. (We might have worn jeans so tight you had to pull up the zipper with a pair of pliers, but we topped them with chunky sweaters big enough to smuggle a fully grown Labrador retriever inside.) My personal wardrobe choices have always been relatively conservative, but STILL. This is just ridiculous.

Is it too much to ask that there be ONE PAIR OF SHORTS in the girls' section of Major Retailers that is long enough to cover the entirety of a girl's natural curves? Sandwiches at Subway are longer than these shorts. We went nuts trying to find a pair that were longer than your standard pair of underwear. After a few tries in different places, we ended up at Wal-Mart, where we did find some Jordache jeans shorts that went down to mid-thigh, and were high enough not to show anything usually only seen on plumbers and electricians. (Once again – let's hear it for the 80s! Our fashions were funky, comfortable, and covered the entirety of our no-no zones, even if our hair wouldn't all fit in the rectangle of our yearbook pictures.) Seriously: it appears that Wal-Mart is the only place I can find clothes with any class. Think about that for a moment.

Not to jump too hard on the feminist Crazy Train, but exactly what are we telling little girls if this is more or less the only clothing option for them? I mean, turn the tables and that would highlight how ridiculous the whole thing is. If a guy were to wear leggings without the benefit of a shirt that went to his thighs, nearly everyone would freak out regarding the bumps and fleshy bits that would be outlined in 3-D. Any guy wearing a Speedo outside of competitive swimming would be ridiculed, or at the very least stared at in a "beware of psycho predator" way. Booty shorts for guys are so ridiculous a concept that there was an entire character based around that joke of a theory on Reno 911. So I don't think it is a double standard in which we are more concerned with what girls wear than what boys wear. It is more like a double standard in which boys are encouraged to wear comfortable, practical clothing that leaves a good bit to the imagination, and girls are encouraged to wear clothes that reveal as much as is legally possible.

I took a completely non-scientific poll of men/guys I know and who happened to cross my path during the period of time when I was most hot under the collar about this. All of them over the age of 18 said that they actually preferred the way females looked when there was a little more coverage, as it was more mysterious and classy. The ones under the age of 18 said the same thing, but they wouldn't look me in the eye and blushed a little when they said it, and maybe typed 5318008 on the calculator to look busy while they were talking. (Try it – and turn the calculator upside down.) Which goes to prove nothing, except maybe that the older men get the more mature they get, either in their taste in women's clothing or in their ability to lie to me convincingly.

Despite the fact that I'm fairly certain my 10 year old's fashion goals don't include "sexy" or "picking up guys for a fling," I'm also aware how often her friends talk about going on a diet and 'thigh gaps' and the relative physical attractiveness of their peers and the latest boy band clones. I don't pretend to have any solutions, or even a clear handle on the problem – I mean, if I'm going to be honest here, if I had long, muscular legs that looked like my daughter's I would show every square inch of them every day for the express purpose of making you cry with jealousy. So maybe I'm just a hypocrite. Who knows?

I guess all I can say after an exhausting rant like this is, to whomever the clerk was at T.J. Maxx upon whom I unleashed just a little bit of a tantrum, I know you're not in charge of these decisions and I apologize for forcing you to deal with my crazy raving when there wasn't a thing you could do about it. But seriously – you weren't wearing booty shorts when I asked where the non-streetwalker section was for little girls. So why do you expect my daughter to?

Milestones

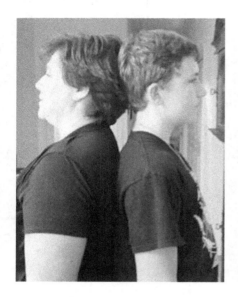

My kids are now 10 and 12, which means that I've been through a lot of significant milestones with them. From learning to smile, to finding out that their feet are actually attached to their bodies, to learning to read, to potty training, to riding a bike and roller skating, to first girlfriends, to (gasp) middle school: my kids and I have been through a lot. I have to say, though, not the first smile, not the first "Mama," nothing came close to freaking me out quite as much as the one we reached this morning. Like most big milestones, this one happened by accident and by surprise. I am 5'6", which puts me on the tall side of average, or maybe the short side of tall. I'm taller than most of my friends, but not all of them. Yesterday, I was taller than my son. Today, I am not.

I have been trying, without success, to institute a "No talking to Mommy until she has finished an entire cup of coffee" rule. This morning, I was trying to enforce this rule while Jacob was what I call "up in my grill." Jacob and the concept of personal space are not friends. I'm not even sure they are acquainted, though Lord knows I've tried my best to get them to meet. I looked up at him to say, "Please, buddy, just a half cup of coffee to go," and then realized I was, in fact, looking up at him.

I knew this day was coming. An early bloomer, his voice changed completely and totally about six months ago. His voice is now indistinguishable from his father's. When I call the house, or when one of them calls me, I often have to wait for one of them to call me "Mommy" or some other context clue to figure out which one I am speaking to. (An aside: "What's for dinner?" does not tell me which one I am talking to.) I'm embarrassed to admit that I can't tell them apart, so I don't ask. I expect my son will be tall. His father is six feet, and my father is six feet, so he gets it from both sides, genetics-wise. I've known for a while this was unavoidable, and I know tall guys have it easier in every way, except, I guess, if they want to be jockeys, so I want him to be tall. So why don't I like this?

Of course, it is entirely possible that he is not only growing, but I am shrinking. I know for a fact that I am taller in the morning, and shorter in the evening, after the work day has literally beaten me down. I know this is true because I have to adjust the rear view mirrors in my car accordingly. My mother for most of my life was taller than me by a hair or two – now she is a good three inches shorter. I remember my grandmother, my mother's mother, as a tiny thing. I towered over her and wore bigger clothes and shoes sometime around fifth or sixth grade. I remember being an older teenager, and for some reason or another I looked at her driver's license, which said she was 5'6". "Grandma!" I said. "Five foot six? Really?"

She got a sad look in her eye and said, "I used to be."

I can't remember if I thought a variant on "Baloney" or if I actually thought it out loud, but until I began to see my own mother vanish into the carpet nap before my eyes, I didn't believe it.

Back a hundred years ago when I turned thirty, it didn't really depress me. I was glad to be turning thirty, because by then I'd been a lawyer for six years already, and I thought if I wasn't in my twenties any more people might start taking me seriously. My mother, on the other hand, was mortified. She did not want me discussing my birthday. If it were up to her, she wouldn't have acknowledged it at all. Because only an old woman could have a thirty year old daughter, and she was having no part of that. Maybe I'm just in denial about the passage of time. I spent so many years being the youngest in the room, that it surprises me to find out how much older I am than other people.

This boy in my house – the one with enough hair on his toes that my daughter calls him Bilbo Baggins – is the same little boy that used to call blueberries "boo-babies" and bananas "manomaneys," and is the same 6 ½ pound newborn whose legs were so skinny even the preemie diapers left gaps around his thighs. His whole torso was as big as my (admittedly man-sized) hand – laying my hand on his chest, I could reach neck to crotch and side to side. Now his hands are bigger than mine. Such is the way of the world, and there isn't any point in fighting it or even being sad about it. Still, feelings aren't always rational, and these are no exception. I know this much though: no matter how tall or big he grows, no matter how low his voice gets, or how thick the mustache that is now just one or two wispy hairs can grow, he'll always be my sweet little boy, and I'll always be his Mommy. Besides which, I will always be meaner, and can make him wither with that mommy-look that I hope will never stop terrifying him. And the taller he is, the more useful he is, able to lift any object off a high shelf and open jars. Soon enough he'll be old enough to drive and I can retire from chauffeur duty.

Now that I think about it, yeah. This is a pretty good day.

The Changing of the Guard

There is a man child living in my house. I don't mean the tall one with grey hair and a pension, I mean the 12-almost-13 year old who is recently grown taller than me, and whose voice is lower than his father's. Of course, the grey-headed one is a man child, too, but for different reasons.

I'm not the only one freaked out by how much and how fast he is growing. It's like the changing of the guard around here, and it is kind of fun to watch. Today, for example, the Mowing of the Lawn was a rather large to-do. My husband, Mike, the grey-headed man child, has recently had back surgery. This makes a lot of tasks that are normally on his list, like mowing the lawn, difficult. Jacob, the younger man child, is perfectly capable of mowing the lawn and, perfectly willing to mow the lawn, go figure, only he doesn't ever do it because of the clash of wills that occur from the Alpha Dog asserting his dominance over the young whelp who will one day take his place. At least that's how I see it. Mike will tell you it is because of Jacob's bad attitude, and Jacob will tell you it is because Mike is an overly-critical control freak. They're both right.

I myself am perfectly capable of mowing the lawn. I did it for years before I got married and one of the lawnmowers we have is still the one I got for $50.00 at a scratch and dent sale sometime in 1996 from Home Depot. I bought it because the one I owned previously was stolen from where I had it chained up to my fence. When I bought the new one, I got some neon paint and painted "Lori's Mower – do not steal" and my address on the mower. The paint is still there, even though I haven't owned that house for thirteen years.

Mike was still in bed resting his back, when Jacob and I announced to him that we were going to mow the lawn so he didn't have to worry about it. He immediately gave us a list of instructions. "Pick up the sticks first. You can use the wheelbarrow or that garbage can we keep outside or I think it is easier to get the garbage can outside and drag it around because it is easier to move the big sticks in it. You can get the rake and just rake the sticks around the outside and scoot them into the woods or the lake. Move the car so you don't blow dirt all over it. The lawnmower is hard to start. I'm probably going to have to start it for you." I kissed him, thanked him for worrying about us, but assured him that we were perfectly capable human beings who could successfully accomplish a simple task like mowing the lawn. After all, it wasn't exactly lush sod we were mowing. It was dirt patches and clover and crab grass, with the occasional lonely, hopeful remnant of fescue poking through.

There had been a storm recently, and great big sticks that might more accurately be called logs filled wheelbarrow after wheelbarrow and got dumped in an area of sticks I call the snake pit. When it was clear enough, Jacob went out to the shed to get to the lawnmower. He announced that there was a newly found type of creature in the shed, some kind of enormous freaky cricket/spider antenna-sporting critter that was eating a smaller spider. But, like the man he is becoming, he did not run away squealing, just kept his distance, and wheeled out the lawn mower. He started it on the first pull and started to mow the perimeter of the yard. I kept picking up sticks and pine cones and hickory nuts so they wouldn't come flying out of the exit chute and impale anyone. Mike came out, and expressed hurt surprise that the lawn mower cranked without his necessary intervention.

Every once in a while I would stop and look up at my sweaty boy, arm and shoulder muscles straining as he pushed the ancient, rusty mower up the slope of the yard, and my heart would try to leap out of my chest with pride. I also wondered when he actually got arm and shoulder muscles. Wasn't it last week that he was a six and a half pound peanut who was soft and squishy everywhere? I have a picture of Jacob, at maybe four or five days old, snuggled on his father's broad chest, his whole curled up body not even reaching from sternum to belly button. Mike, at the time, had more pepper than salt in his hair.

I'm not sure what I think: in turns pride and sadness and love and true wonder, about the ascent to power of one of my men and the waning strength of the other. I love them both. I'm proud of them both. Even when they lock horns and try to throw each other off the side of the mountain.

Happy Birthday To Me

This year, on my birthday, I turned 44. I'm at an age where I've got a while to go before any kind of milestone birthdays, and I'm just sort of a boring, in the middle of my life age with nothing much to recommend it or dislike about it. This drives my kids nuts. They believe their birthdays to be national holidays, and cannot believe that I could meet one with a noncommittal "Meh."

This year, my birthday came six days after my husband's back surgery, so I didn't expect much out of the day beyond a phone call from my parents and a bunch of Facebook messages. I was not disappointed or surprised, pleasantly or otherwise.

It wasn't until about 1:00 pm that anyone in my family even remembered that it was my birthday. Since we had no cake in the house, or appropriate candles, my son shoved a half-used taper candle in a hot dog bun, lit it, and sang happy birthday. He then got offended that I did not eat the wax covered bun with gusto. My daughter, not to be outdone then wrapped up a pretty glass paperweight she had in her room and gave it to me. My husband, still coming off the anesthesia and on a steady diet of painkillers, said something incoherent about Dr. Bruce needing the VCR tapes and went back to bed.

Later that day, I had the pleasure of dropping my son off at band camp for a week. Jacob kept apologizing that I had to spend my birthday toting him across the state and dragging his duffel bag up four flights of stairs after shelling out $40.00 for the DVD of a concert that hasn't even happened yet. (No elevator? Really? Isn't that an ADA violation or something?) I didn't care. Really, didn't care.

Really.

And then I did. Not so much about the band camp thing, because that couldn't be helped. It was more the fact that the best that anyone could scare up was a stale, waxy hot dog bun and a used paperweight. That night, my daughter had a friend sleep over and my husband stayed in La La Land in our bedroom. I stole away to the back porch where I attempted to give myself a birthday present, twenty minutes of sitting in silence in the hammock chair reading a book. I knew it was getting late, and I knew someone had to deal with the topic of dinner, but I just didn't feel like it. Marin and her friend, who spends so much time at my house she might as well live here, came out every few minutes and asked me what was for dinner. I told them to chill out, and I'd get to it eventually. Around eight o'clock they began to get suspicious that it wasn't really going to happen, and told me so. In a burst of self pity borne from the fact that I couldn't even give MYSELF a successful birthday present (time on the hammock without being bothered) I barked, "It's MY birthday! Why do *I* have to make dinner?" Marin's friend apologized and swore she didn't know what day it was. Marin just kind of backed away slowly.

And so, the girls set to work, banishing me from the kitchen into my bedroom. They were going to bake a cake, but discovered that we had no cake or cake mix, or any kind of ingredients they could turn into a cake on their own. They came into my room, heads hung with failure. I mentioned that we did have pancake mix, and perhaps they could use that and some blueberries to come up with something. After some banging and chatter and some burnt smells, I was told perhaps pancakes weren't such a great idea, and they'd make popsicles instead, only they probably wouldn't be ready until tomorrow, so would I mind waiting.

I didn't mind waiting. I didn't mind that the next day the girls ate the popsicles they made themselves. It just made me happy that for a little bit someone tried to do something nice for me. That for a small slice of time my well being and my pleasure was the focus of some other human beings.

Isn't that all any of us want? Well, that and a tropical vacation and a genie who grants unlimited wishes. (But only the kind you're not sorry you make…..I've read enough of those fairy tales to know to be careful of what I wish for…..)

Woman Stuff

Compressed Fat

There isn't much we can agree on as a society, but I think we can all safely agree on this: women's body fat is much lumpier than men's body fat. Overweight men tend to have round bellies and rounded arms. Overweight women have lumps and bumps in random places. There are no straight or gently curved lines. Instead, we have random pockets of fat, peaks and valleys and cratered landscapes, without the benefit of fashionable tent-like clothing to cover it up.

This might sound suspiciously like complaining. And, although it is reason number 4,527,291 on the long list of reasons why in our society it is easier to be a man, I am at this moment merely observing and being descriptive. I promise.

A good number of women will tell you that along with penicillin and automatic dishwashers and airplanes and GPS, one of the greatest inventions of the 20th century was the product known as "Spanx". For a while, Spanx was the only game in town, now there are lots of similar competitors. Spanx is, for the blissfully uninformed, the modern incarnation of the girdle. They come in different lengths and colors, but the basic idea is that they are shaped like shorts (more like the top part of pantyhose) and compact all the gooey, lumpy fat into a smooth package. Kind of like compression shorts. So while the extra load still may be more rounded than you want it to be, at least it is simply rounded and not all bumpy like a gravel road after a meteor shower.

Of course, no product is perfect, and no product can replace the only diet which works long term, in my estimation, the 'eat less and exercise more' diet. And no diet will help some of the genetic realities of the female form. So while there are certain pants and skirts that I own that I cannot wear in public without the assistance of the above-described supportive undergarments, these fat squeezers aren't perfect.

The legs give me the greatest grief. Although I do have a lot of muscle in my thighs, the muscles are protected by an insulated layer of cushy fat. This means that the bottom of the leg of the Spanx, where the compression ends, has a bit of a bulge underneath it where the uncompressed fat breathes a sigh of relief that it has not had to be squished all day. If I am wearing skinny-ish pants this makes for a bizarre looking thigh line. But even in a skirt or roomier pants, this happy fat talks to its oppressed fat sisters above the line of demarcation between smooth/not smooth and the oppressed sisters rebel and demand to be set free. This results in a gradual crawling upwards of the bottom of the shorts, so that by the end of the day they are rolled up into miniature inner tubes nestled between my thigh and hip. Sometimes, if I am retaining water or my belly swells with a celebratory lunch for someone's birthday and a slice of cake (since we all know that to turn down birthday cake is an Unforgiveable Sin which will result in Bad Luck for Ten Generations,) the top elastic gives up standing proud and starts crawling down the slope of my gut. This is a creepy feeling, and only seems to occur when I am doing something formal, like presenting a case in court, or speaking to a client. Sometimes it happens so fast it startles me and I make weird, jerky movements which are awkward to explain. (I usually just say "mosquito" and no one questions me.) It is an easily fixable problem, but I can't always find the time to fix it, so an unreasonable amount of brain power in professional situations is spent pretending like I don't feel my underwear crawling down my body.

Reading over this, it all looks ridiculous. Why on Earth do I and my many friends do this to ourselves? Probably the same reason we pluck hairs out of our body one by one or en masse with hot wax; the same reason we put sharpened pencils filled with grease paint a sixteenth of an inch from our actual eyeballs; and the same reason we are expected to both bring home the bacon AND fry it up in a pan: life ain't fair. Get used to it.

Sensible Shoes

I have very large feet. Feet so large that I have trouble finding shoes that fit me in normal stores, and keep thinking I need to find a store that caters to drag queens. This is in keeping with my 'generally large' body type. When I grew to my full height (5'6") at the ripe old age of 12, and had size 11 wide feet, and hands almost as big as my father's, my doctor declared that I would likely be 5 foot 9 or 10. Ha ha. Although my weight is appropriate for someone who is 5 foot 10, I remain, more or less, the same size that I was in sixth grade.

But back to my feet. In addition to being the length and width of snowshoes, they are perfectly flat, prone to bunions, and I have this weird toe thing going on that my grandmother had, that makes my second toe on my left foot ache and burn unless I wear these things that feel like giant (soothing) lumps in my shoes.

And yet, I am a woman. Which means, stereotypically, that I like shoes. I like cute shoes. I like heels that give the illusion that I am tall enough for my weight and my legs aren't quite so short and stubby. I like heels that make my calves look they have muscles. Except that one time I interviewed with Governor Sonny Purdue and I wore four inch heels and no one told me that would make me taller than him. That was a mistake. (I didn't get the job.)

It was years after bunion surgery before I finally gave up the ghost. It started slowly, when I decided I would only wear heels that had a little strap across the front so that I wouldn't have to keep my toes all crampy curled to keep the shoes on while I walked down stairs or across a room or something. Then I discovered what I called "orthopedic heels." These are shoes that cost as much as my car that aren't quite as cute, but still don't look like I got them at a nursing home gift shop, and are actually cushioned and supportive and foot shaped. I decided I would transition, as finances allow, to two pair of orthopedic heels per season in two basic colors, black and brown. So now I own four pairs of heels. Two winter, two summer.

And I'm even thinking of giving that up. Fashion be damned. Who am I kidding anyway? I'm really really married. I really really have two kids. Who am I trying to impress? I have enough things getting in my way of getting things done without adding the distraction of aching feet to the mix. And besides, the more dress-up occasions I go to where I am wearing heels and my husband complains that his dress shoes (which are flat, foot-shaped, wide, and have laces for adjustable custom fit) hurt his feet, the more danger he is of ending up in the emergency room with a three-inch stiletto sticking out of his forehead.

All of which is an incredibly long introduction to the following observation: I recently visited Universal Studios Orlando with my family. While there, I wore practical shorts with deep pockets, t-shirts, and athletic socks and sneakers. I wore no makeup and brushed, but didn't fix my hair in any way. I know that I looked like dumpy middle-aged suburban Mom, complete with my plaid tourist shorts and lanyard around my neck containing my "Express Pass" and "Star Photo Card". I wasn't trying to look cute. I was trying to have the appropriate parts covered, be functional, and keep track of my children. So it isn't fair to compare me to the cute, skinny 18-25 demographic prancing around with their boyfriends. But really. I saw so many girls (and yes, everyone with such poor decision making ability is a 'girl' as I define the word) wearing mini skirts and heels. Heels. Heels! In what universe is that a good idea? We walked 724 miles each day, and that was just to get to the first ride, not counting standing in line for 45 minutes to ride it. Wearing my running shoes with the orthotic inserts, my legs were shaky and achy by lunchtime. I cannot imagine making it past the front gate in heels without ending up in tears and with a permanent limp, and possibly a severed artery.

Some women were still so image conscious that even being over 30 and sometimes with kids they were wearing cute leopard print flats with pointy toes or sparkles. Shoes that were made to look good, not distance walk in or stand in for more than 10 minutes. Once I noticed this, I couldn't not notice it. Very few women were wearing sneakers or traditional walking shoes. A lot of them were wearing flip flops, which I will grant you are better than dress flats or heels, but still not distance walking shoes. Men, on the other hand, all wore either sneakers, boat shoes, or flip flops. Not a pointy toe or stacked heel to be found.

So what it all boils down to is this: we can choose to look cute or we can minimize the pain in our lives. Alternatively, we middle aged folks, with our buying power and influence, can demand that shoes that don't require our foot to be squeezed into shapes not found in nature be considered the height of fashion. "Manshoes for the fall! Now in silver sparkle and pumpkin suede!"

Meh. Who am I kidding? Those yellow patent leather shoes with the cork heels are too cute. Do you think they come in an 11 wide?

Baby Brain

Two babies came into my office today. Not at the same time, and each accompanied by a very affectionate and seemingly competent mother. These were exceptionally cute babies, each only 11 months old, and oozing with wordless personality. The mothers were there to transact business. Me? As much as I wanted to transact business, as transacting business is how I earn a living, I was completely unable to form thoughts more coherent than, "Lookit that smile! Yes! You're a big boy, aren't you?"

Back before I had any babies of my own, I had this near-psychotic, clearly biological urge to have one. I could smell a baby within 100 yards, and would run to it, begging to hold it. Once in my arms, I would bury my nose in the top of their velvety heads and smell that unique baby smell of powder, milk, Desitin, spitup, and poop, and I would think, "one day...."

Then I had my own. After my son was born, I knew for absolute certain (even on those nights when I fantasized about leaving him in his crib with a few bottles and driving off into the sunset) that I wanted another one. I was fortunate enough to have my daughter two years later. After that, as much as I knew I wanted babies to begin with, I knew I did not want another one. Two was my limit.

Now, when I see a baby, after my biological alarm clock rang and got snoozed and finally turned off for good, I still want to feel its soft baby skin and make an absolute fool out of myself to be rewarded with a smile. But I'm happy enough to give it back to its mother/father/grandparents/foster parents/ babysitter after a few minutes. Thank God I don't have one of those, I think, but holey moley they are cute.

There are six women who work in my office, and one lonely man, Don. Don't feel too badly for him – he has six daughters and a wife, so he actually cuts down on the number of women telling him what to do by coming in to work. Three of us (not me! Yay!) have daughters young enough to be considered babies or toddlers themselves. One of us has a new grandkid every year, the oldest being seven. So there are a lot of babies that show up in our office from time to time.

Whenever this happens, odd things happen to us. Between the six women, there are twenty-eight years of post-secondary education. That's a pretty well educated bunch. All of us have our own children. And yet, at the merest whiff of Desitin, our voices raise an octave and a half, and we have to cease writing briefs and advising clients about life changing issues in order to fight for the right to say, "Aaaaaaahbooboobooobooobooo" right into the face of a very young human whose ability to converse starts and ends with "dadadadada."

Don seems generally oblivious to the presence of babies, and goes about his business as if there weren't this snuggly, warm little IQ-reducing presence in the office. I think the only thing he notices is that the rest of us are completely useless.

Why is this? There are lots of cute things in the world that I can merely note as cute in my brain without feeling the need to manhandle it or stop what I'm doing to observe. I don't *have* to hold someone's puppy. I don't feel the need to dangle string in front of a kitty's face. When I do play with puppies and kittens, I still manage to speak in a manner befitting a middle aged woman with a law degree.

I guess it is the helplessness of babies. Once weaned, kittens and puppies can survive on their own, for the most part. They are hard wired to find scraps of food to eat and chase mice. They poop and pee where they please (outdoors) with no consequence. Even little kittens are instinctively drawn to a litter box. Baby humans are completely helpless. For the first year of their lives they do precious little but take – quite literally like leaches. It was stunning to me to realize how little my children knew and how little they were capable of doing when they were born. My son had a cold when he was about six weeks old, and his inability to sniff or blow or recognize that he could breathe out of his mouth by choice made his suffering much more intense. (And, I admit, hilarious. Yeah, I'm the kind of parent who took a video of that sort of thing.)

Jumping right into stereotypes, women seem to be hardwired to gravitate towards the helpless. It is our job, whether or not we want it to be, and whether or not we resent the heck out of it, to make sure that what everyone in our orbit needs is taken care of. We are capable of recognizing that "waaaaaaaah!" means I'm hungry, and "WAHWAHWAH" means a wet diaper and "waaaaaaaahWAHWAHwaaaaaaaah" means I'm sleepy. My husband was always mystified that I could interpret my children's cries. I was always mystified that he couldn't. He is still mystified that I can look at my children in the morning and predict that they will be sick later in the day.

I'm not sure why any of this is, but I challenge you to disagree with me with concrete examples rather than theory. In the meantime, since there are no babies about, I'd better get some work done while I am still capable of rational thought.

Bad Hair Day

One day the people in charge of fashion will decide that bald women look amazing, and I will be the first person in line to shave my head. I have never actually seen my uncovered scalp. I was born with hair and have never been without it, but a tactile examination reveals my skull to be full of lumps and bumps and crevasses and flat plains. So that probably wouldn't be pretty even if bald theoretically was. Plus, if I were bald I'd be slathering the top of my head with sunscreen all the time so I wouldn't end up looking like you could fry an egg up there. But a girl can dream.

On the one hand, I have a full head of plentiful hair, and, at the ripe old age of 43 it still grows in a consistent dark brown, the color of muddy topsoil. So there's that, and I suppose I should be grateful. On the other hand, my hair is so oily that approximately 22 hours after I last washed it, it looks like I dipped my head in a deep fryer. It also either completely defies gravity or obeys it intensely. In other words, its entire length is either clinging to my head as if it might fall out if it let go, or sticking up in completely random directions. Sometimes you will find patches of each on different parts of my head. This also happens when I sleep, even if I took a 15 minute cat nap while sitting up in a chair or if I took a shower right before I went to bed.

When I use product and a quarter can of hair spray as per my work day routine, this isn't really a problem, since it will hold during the work day and people don't usually see me after

8pm. On weekends, however, I spend inordinate amounts of time finding ways to make it look socially acceptable. (This is not to be confused with looking *good*. I don't care if I look *good*. I just want to look like I did whatever it looks like on *purpose*.)

Wetting my hair doesn't work, it just rearranges the patches of cling and spike. Occasionally that dry shampoo stuff does work, but as it is basically jet-propelled white rice powder, I look like I'm about to play George Washington in the school play. Headbands don't work, because if I tame the front with one, the back end has a little fork-in-a-light-socket party to make up for it. Rather than making me look glamorous like Audrey Hepburn, scarves have a tendency to make me look I am undergoing chemotherapy. (I have loads of sympathy for the women going through chemotherapy, and find a great deal of beauty in their strength, but no one I'm aware of considers the side effects a desirable fashion choice.) Bandanas make it look like I am here to clean your house. Hats are ok, but I have a head the size of a seedless watermelon, and most women's hats don't fit me. Regular ball caps just look odd and manly on top of most of the clothes I wear. Smaller, more 'feminine' caps just kind of perch on my head like I'm wearing a hat made for an American Girl Doll.

The easy answer, of course, is to just jump in the shower, which is what I do most of the time. It's not that I'm anti-hygiene, but shouldn't I be able to have a lazy sweat pants Saturday morning and run my daughter to her Girl Scout meeting without primping? And what about the days where I know in two hours I am going to go swimming in the lake? Should

I wash it and blow dry it just to have it covered in lake muck 90 minutes later? And what about those times when I take a shower at the end of the day, whether it is because I am sweaty from the gym, or just want to wash off the day before I sleep it off? Should I really have to take *another* shower in the morning just so it looks like I'm not heading off to my final exam at clown college?

I'm not asking you like you might have an answer for me. Not that you aren't full of good ideas, but I'm well aware that there isn't a good answer. Truthfully, what I really ought to do is invest some money in a quality, good-looking wig, and just plop it on my military grade buzz cutted head every morning looking exactly the same.

So maybe that's what I will do. You'll know if I do it because I will start looking good on Saturday mornings and weekday evenings. I would say let's keep it our little secret, but I know me better than that. I'll sing it from the rafters, and look down on people who bother with their own hair. Why bother? I will ask. Fake is the new real.

The Banned Articles

Author's Note: Most of these chapters started out as blog posts or columns for either the Patch or Your Local News. Before I publish any of them, I run them by my screening committee, which consists of two wonderful women named Diane Hale and Linda Oulton. Linda is a great editor, and Diane tends to be what I call my "Southern Baptist Conscience." These are useful things, because awkward syntax, grammatical mistakes, and typos are evil, but they happen to the best of us; also, as someone who is Jewish and raised by unrepentant Yankees in the north, I often have no clue what will offend my local readers. I live in the semi-rural south, smack in the heart of the Bible Belt, about 45 minutes east of Atlanta. To say the sensibilities here are different from the sensibilities of my parents and the general population where I grew up would be akin to saying that diamonds are different from Jell-O brand instant chocolate pudding powder. I'm not interested in offending anyone or making anyone uncomfortable. I know I need my screening committee. I am a lawyer in a small town and I need to be a relatively well respected member of the community in order to continue to get business and referrals. Truly, I'm never sure if these get vetoed because they are offensive in some way, or because the reveal the depth of my insanity, which ought to be kept deep down near the Earth's core. So my screening committee is great. They save me from me.

In fact, "Banned" is probably a strong word, I still don't cuss or describe sex in detail, but "I wouldn't if I were you, that's not ladylike" isn't as snappy a title.

Still.

I get older and older and care less and less about what other people think about what I have to say. Besides, the following are some of my favorites. I hope you like them, too. If you think I'm crude or nuts, don't blame it on Linda or Diane.

Passive Listening

I want to pose a question: Is there anything on Earth more trying of one's patience than passive listening? I probably shouldn't put this out there, but if you ever want to get information out of me, and I'm not talking, avoid water boarding or anything else specifically recognized by the Geneva Convention. No. Put me somewhere in which I am required to be well behaved and do nothing other than listen to someone speaking in a monotone FOR LONG PERIODS OF TIME. For these purposes, I'm going to define "Long Periods of Time" as anything longer than seven minutes in a row. Put me in a knee length skirt so that I have to keep my knees together. Put me in an uncomfortable chair so I have to sit up straight. Don't allow me to roll my eyes or otherwise facially express my opinion. Don't let me close my non-rolling eyes. I will tell you anything, and might give you a kidney or a child if you will just make the droning stop.

I am truly dangerous in these situations. Anything is possible. If there were anyone who could read my thoughts at these times, I would immediately be taken away into an ambulance by those nice, young men in their clean, white coats. That's not necessarily a bad thing. I don't mean to diminish true mental illness, but *man* the thought of a thirty day stay in a place where the tranquilizers flow freely, everything is painted in soothing, pastel colors, and everyone speaks in soft voices is appealing.

I have been blessed with the ability to type very quickly. I am fluent enough with a keyboard that I can take near-transcripted notes on a laptop while someone is talking. To make things better, I can do this while my brain is absolutely elsewhere. Oh, and elsewhere it goes.

There is usually a predictable pattern to this. The first thing that happens is my skeleton gets jumpy. Tired of being in a formal pose, it tries to jump out of my skin. This makes for a game that entertains me for upwards of three or four minutes. I practice my poker face. I try to see how still and how passive my face and body can be while inside my bones are trying to jump on the table and flamenco dance just to break up the monotony. They are screaming, "Let me out! Let me out!" as loudly as they can, while I sit, arranging my face as carefully as I can into a neutral pose, trying to muffle the noise in my brain with only the power of my thoughts.

Eventually, my skeleton loses hope and I try to rationalize my way out of despair. This isn't so bad, I think. How long can it possibly go? 'Til 5pm? 6? That's only (I look at my watch) six hours from now. Six hours. That's not so long. People survive for years in POW camps, and at least I know I'll be sleeping in my own bed tonight and it is highly unlikely that anyone will hit me with the butt of a pistol or chain my wrists so high I have to stand on tip-toe. What can I do in six hours? Oh, only 75% of the backlog of paperwork on my desk. I could clean all my bathrooms and mop the floors and vacuum the carpet and de-funk the microwave and still have time to read a few chapters in a book. I could watch the first three Harry Potter movies with my obsessed daughter. I could drive all the way to Panama City with enough time to stop twice to go potty and get a snack. I could (and here is where I start shouting silently)

SIT ON MY SOFA AND PICK MY NOSE WHICH WOULD
BE INFINITELY MORE PRODUCTIVE AND ENJOYABLE
THAN LISTENING TO THIS MORON GO ON AND ON
AND ON ABOUT BLAH BLAH BLAH. DOES HE REALLY
THINK ANYONE IS LISTENING? DOES HE LIKE THE
SOUND OF HIS VOICE OH SO VERY MUCH? DOES HE
NOT THINK THAT IF YOU ARE GOING TO TALK TO
SOMEONE FOR MORE THAN 90 SECONDS THAT YOU
HAVE A MORAL OBLIGATION TO AT LEAST *TRY* TO BE
ENTERTAINING?

Then the thoughts start getting a little more graphic. I
imagine myself thrusting my chair backwards while I spring
up, shouting, "Oh, for the love of all that is good and holy, shut
your mouth. Just shut up. SHUT UP! Why? Why are you
still talking? Do you not know that everyone in this room has
pictured themselves cutting off your oxygen with your own tie
just to make it stop?" I picture myself using the tie as a noose
while his face gets bluer and bluer and his eye start to bug out,
and everyone else in the audience is cheering and……..

At that point my own imagination usually scares me sufficiently that I try to go to my happy place. My happy place is
Lake Oconee, floating on my back with the sunshine kissing
my face. In the near distance my children are playing joyfully.
The only thing I can hear with any clarity is the water slap-
slap-slapping against the logs of the pontoon boat making a
wonderful hollow sproingy gong sound that can only be associ-
ated with happy times.

I can only keep up this illusion for so long, though, since
the truth is that it is an extremely mellow image and I'm not

that mellow of a person. So then I start playing little mental games, like writing parodies of songs. For example, right now I am working on a twist on an oldie-but-goodie from Sir Mix-A-Lot which I am calling, "I like big boats." "I like big boats and I cannot lie, you other mothers can't deny, when a ship pulls in with an itty-bitty head and a motor that ain't dead you get WILD! Wanna pull up tough cuz you know that boat was stuffed deep in the lake she's skiing, I'm hooked and I can't stop" Peeing? Bleeding? Seething? Around this point I get stuck and I am reminded that this guy is still talking. He's still talking! Isn't he boring himself? Argh! I picture myself grabbing him by the throat and......

Calm down, girl, calm down. This will end. This, too, shall pass, just like everything else. Breathe deep, breathe slowly. Be grateful for your health, be grateful for your scads of self-discipline that prevent you from ever ever ever acting out on any of these horrible fantasies. Be grateful for your ability to drive yourself to this boring lecture, be grateful for your husband and your children, and ...

I really have to go to the bathroom. The only thing I can think of is my aching bladder and the fact that this guy is preventing me from relieving myself. I look at my watch. It has only been 45 minutes since the last time I went to the women's room. Will anyone notice if I go again this soon? Will they think I'm pregnant? Will they think I'm faking? Do I care? Oh, Lord, I think I'm going to wet myself if I don't go right this very instant. I hate being this hyper-aware of my waste-removal organs, and I start wondering if anyone else is thinking about theirs which makes *me* think about theirs. Oh, this is bad. This is very bad. What would happen if I just stood up and dropped my pants and relieved myself on the conference room table just to liven things up? This ridiculous image usually makes me want to giggle, and the next ten minutes or so are spent digging my fingernails into my palm or biting my lips and tongue just to feel something that will distract me from the overwhelming desire to laugh a deep belly laugh for no reason more than the pleasure of it.

I have always been surprised that there is this much shouting and chaos going on in my head and no one ever seems to hear it. I think maybe I really should take up poker if I can suppress that much. In the meantime, please, if you ever find yourself speaking to a group of people, and, more importantly, if I am in your audience, do your best to be interesting and take frequent breaks. Your physical safety in the fantasies of other people depends upon it.

Supportive Undergarments

As I sit here wondering if it is in fact possible to be stabbed to death with an underwire, I have to also wonder why we put up with wearing the blamed things in the first place. I will grant you they are infinitely superior to whalebone corsets that had to be tied by your maidservant who braced herself with a foot in the small of your back to get the laces extra tight. Women didn't faint all the time back then because they were weak and sensitive. They fainted because their rib cages were bound tightly so they couldn't breathe, and were covered head to toe in layers of fabric in 100 degree heat without air conditioning or even readily available ice water. Plus, if you weren't expected or allowed to say or do anything in a stressful situation for fear of being seen as unladylike, wouldn't it be awfully convenient to remove yourself from the room with a fake swoon? I tell ya, there are plenty of days in which I wish I could get away with that.

So undoubtedly we have made improvements. But in these days, where wearing shorts and a t-shirt is perfectly acceptable for most American women, when nothing but a glass ceiling stops us from achieving our goals, why do we strap up our girls with metal bones? The same reason we pluck hairs and wear makeup and heels and all manner of stuff guys wouldn't consider doing.

I will grant you that a well constructed contraption of a bra does plenty for us full figured gals. They lift, they separate, they better balance our hips and do in fact make us look better according to conventional American standards. The girls should be front and center and facing forwards as we face our day. No one will disagree with me here.

But WHY? We aren't the only gender with dangly parts. Why must only women defy gravity and strap 'em up? It isn't that there is a blanket rule that everything hanging down should be obviously perky. Can you imagine if guys had to wear supportive undergarments that made their parts stick straight out and face you? And before you start thinking that I am making things up and being ridiculous, I suggest you take a tour of the Arms & Armor collection at the Metropolitan Museum of Art in Manhattan. I went there in high school with some other teenagers, and there are some comically huge metallic bananas curving outwards and upwards from the nether regions on these suits of armor. I want to say that I went with my AP European History class, because I have a vague recollection of the teacher trying to get us to quit giggling by telling us that this was seen as a sign of virility and power, rather than anything sexual. But really? I know times have changed, but I can't imagine that the 13 year old girls in the 1400s or whenever didn't watch the cute boys at jousting practice and giggle behind their fans at the giant silver wiener attached to the front of Lancelot's pants.

So just like corsets and petticoats have made way for underwire bras and Spanx, why haven't there been similar modifications for men? It seems silly now. Seriously, imagine the commercials and ads that would promise lifting and enhancing for men. Why is this not only ok but expected for women's private parts and not men's private parts? Why do we have to pay 80 bucks a pop for well constructed underwear? Can you imagine a single man that would put up with that? And why do we get mad when someone stares at something we have lifted and pointed at their eyeballs? If we don't want them to look, why do we go out of our way to make them obvious?

That's a lot of questions with no good answers.

I'm not saying we need to ditch the concept all together. When I don't wear anything, um, supportive, on lazy weekend mornings (both of those lazy weekend mornings that I have had time to have this year) if I move around too much (read: at all) my back starts to hurt from supporting the weight unassisted. Sudden movements can create g-forces and a painful sudden shifting of weight. I could get a black eye. (Seriously. When I see those women running in slo-mo down the beach on Baywatch, their girl parts boinging in a different tempo and direction than the rest of their bodies, all I think is, "Ow!") So we need something there for comfort's sake. But why not stick to sports bras that smush everything together in an immobile uniboob and allow for unfettered movement? Why not stick to the soft nursing bras that are comfortable enough to sleep in?

I'm not looking to make a political statement with my underwear. I just want to be able to think without a metal half circle gouging a hole in my side because I shifted the wrong way in my chair. People would look funny at me if I started rooting around in my shirt to adjust during a business meeting. There's only so many times you can get up on a fake bathroom trip to adjust your clothing, and odds are good I've already gotten up twice to adjust my Spanx, which have either crept up or down, depending on which the Powers that Be think would irritate me the most.

I remember being a little girl and wishing that I were big and grownup enough to wear a bra like a real lady. I guess it is true: be careful what you wish for. You just might get it.

Excuse Me, Is That Charcoal in Your Pants?

I'm a community minded kind of gal, always looking out for the greater good, and so when I see a product come on to the market that might revolutionize life as we know it, I feel the need to spread the word. Naturally, when I came across an ad for "Flat-D Flatulence Deodorizer" I knew I was looking at one of those products.

The Flat-D Flatulence Deodorizer is essentially a charcoal pad which sticks to one's underwear like a maxipad and filters the odorific gasses that might emit from the place adjacent to where the pad is stuck. Brilliant, I thought. I know quite a few people in my own family that might benefit from the use of these things.

Nothing, however, is as good as it seems at first blush. In my haste to spread the word via social media, I failed to see the entire story. It was pointed out that the inconclusively-gendered model in the ad wore the pad on the outside of his or her white cotton underwear. This would make for some interesting panty lines. It is unclear from the picture or the descriptors in the ad if the adhesive part of the pad has to be facing the, um, exhaust pipe for the charcoal filter to operate properly.

I wanted to know more. I needed to know more. So I went to Amazon.com to see how much the product cost and to read reviews. I learned that the makers of Flat-D Flatulence Deodorizers were not the only makers of this type of revolutionary product. I learned that while the Flat-D pads were adequate, the "Subtle Butt" brand flatulence deodorizer pads were the reviewers' favorite.

Butt wait, there's more.

I also learned that there are other, semi-related products out there which are also useful to the average American. For example, there are a variety of small bottles of hand sanitizers designed to avoid awkward conversations when one sees, for example, one's teenage son who has been sitting on the sofa watching Sports Center reaching into the community bowl of Doritos. This particular bottle is labeled "Maybe You Touched Your Genitals." I'm thinking every guy over the age of, well, six months might want to keep this baby on the little table next to the sofa for easy access.

I know that speaking about flatulence isn't something a lady is supposed to do. But so what? Let's embrace reality instead of pretending it doesn't exist. I posted a link to this product on my Facebook page. One of my more obscure-trivia minded friends pointed out that the average human might, um, have need of one of these pads 16-18 times a day. Another friend followed up with the fact that if you have a balanced diet and healthy levels of coliform bacteria, that you should produce 1-2 cups of gas daily. From these facts I learned that the vast majority of people I am related to are above-average.

When my friends gave me these little tidbits – and who knew that my friends were so knowledgeable about diges- tive mechanics? -- I pointed out that I was pretty sure Queen Elizabeth never once tooted, not even when she was a baby. Same for Grace Kelly, anyone with the title "Dowager

Countess," and most prima ballerinas. (Opera stars, however, I'm pretty sure let it fly.) I know this isn't true – intellectually. I know that due to the hard work of the beneficial bacteria that live in our digestive tract there is a certain amount of air that gets into the tubing, and has to be released in some way or we would look like those 'balloon' animals near the beginning of Shrek when he and Princess Fiona first start to be friends. It is just hard to accept on a gut – ha ha – level.

So let's quit sweeping this natural process under the rug or burying it between the sofa cushions. This stuff happens when we are healthy. Why not advertise our good health? I mean, so long as we have our Flat-D pads strapped securely on.

You start.

Special Bonus Chapter

Author's note: when people ask me about my writing, I usually say that although I have been writing my whole life, I didn't really find my voice until I was in my 40s. It was then that I started writing short, humorous blogs and gave up on the hope that I was capable of writing the Great American Novel. My writing attention span just wasn't that long.

Not long after my first book, Mismatched Shoes and Upside Down Pizza, came out, I was talking to my Dad. He reminded me of an essay I'd written while in high school about back-seat drivers in airplanes. He remembered it being funny. He remembered that it won some kind of award or something. He thought I should include it in my next book. I only vaguely remembered it. I had no idea if I could find it.

When I got home, I looked in the filing cabinet where I keep stuff like that. It was either in there or lost to the ages.

It was in there. Typewritten on a typewriter that smudged the inside of the lowercase e's. But there nonetheless.

I was probably sixteen or so when I wrote this. I was surprised by how much the voice was recognizably the forerunner of my current one, even though it is obviously a Reagan Era commentary, as well as a commentary on watching my parents in the car together. From what little I can recall, we were asked to write a Jonathan Swift-type satire, and this essay was my homework for that assignment.

Dad, this one's for you. Thanks for remembering.

An Alternative To Re-Regulation

It has come to my attention that the once flourishing airline industry now flounders as a result of less careful navigation and air traffic controlling. The newspapers and shows are polluted with horror stories about fatal plane crashes and hair-raising near misses. Just last weekend I read in *The New York Times* of two jumbo jets that flew within thirty feet of each other at nearly five hundred miles an hour. Of *course* this is shattering the confidence of the public. As the odds for death or injury grow less favorable, so shrinks the population of traveling Americans willing to use the airways as their means of transportation.

Many people, including myself, tend to believe that this calamity is due to the recent government deregulation of the industry. They clamor for reregulation, claiming that the standards and rules set by the government would force the industry to "get its act together." While I firmly believe this would work, its drawbacks include forcing our government to swallow its pride, thus lowering its credibility in the eyes of those with whom it wishes to negotiate; and while it does not hurt any aspect of daily life, it will not help any, other than making the airways safe again.

But there is a way to improve safety without having the government resort to this degrading method. I believe I have a suggestion that will not only save the failing industry and make safe airways once again the norm, but improve the unemployment rate, promote the circulation of currency, and promote foreign money to find its way into our economy, thus reducing the trade deficit.

With the invention of the automobile was created an entirely new breed of human being, the notorious "back seat driver" who generally did not sit in the back seat, but rather on the passenger side of the front. These people, by way of screeches, shouts, noises from fright, and even the power of their gaze, have saved many unsuspecting drivers from serious, if not fatal, crashes.

It is at this point that I must admit that I do have a personal gain to be made from my humble suggestion. My mother is, and I may state this without fear of argument, the most skilled backseat driver ever to have graced the face of this Earth. I can recall countless family outings where she has snatched us from the hungry jaws of death by warning my father that the roads were slippery, that he was tailgating, that a red light was impending, or that a car was approaching. I can say in more ways than one that I owe each precious breath to her.

I am not suggesting, however, that these backseat drivers should singlehandedly take over the maneuvering of jumbo jets. Quite the contrary. In fact, these skilled observers tend to be the worst of drivers. My mother's car has been crashed while she was behind the wheel so often that we refer to her car affectionately as the "bumper car." No, these people should remain doing what they do best – observing the conditions around them and advising the pilot of the correct course of action.

And it is thus that I propose that a new form of employment be created in the airline industry – the backseat observer. S/he would sit in the cockpit, and merely guide the plane to safety.

The labor force to fill these positions is readily available, as any harried driver can attest to. While the addition of these people to the payroll of the airlines would force them to raise their prices, I believe the public would be willing to pay a little more for a safer service.

And salary is all the airline would have to pay for. These laborers require no careful training as the pilots and others do. Their skill is inborn, and easily identifiable. One simple, sure-fire test is to ask the applicant how many accidents their spouse has gotten into while they were in the car.

But improved safety is not the only benefit that can be attained from this proposal. The addition of all these people to the workforce will cut down on unemployment. And the greater success of the industry will create a greater need for its services, thus a need for more jobs in the industry, still further reducing unemployment.

And with lowered unemployment comes more money available for spending by the newly employed. This new spending money will soon be circulated throughout our economic system, making it stronger and more stable. With a more stable economic system, the U.S. dollar will gain more weight and rise in value in comparison with other currencies of the free world.

It may sound far fetched, but the steps, followed logically as outlined here, show that this conclusion is inevitable.

The End

The end. Those are really fun words to type for an author. They only come at the end (ha ha) of months of hard work, and they signify a whole lot of other hard work that's different.

Like my last one, I had help on this book.

A hearty thank you once again to everyone who bought Mismatched Shoes and Upside Down Pizza. If you bought more than one, I owe you a drink. If you bought more than two, I owe you a kidney. A kidney AND a cornea if you also reviewed it online somewhere.

Thanks to everyone who visited my website, and double thanks if you bothered signing up for my email newsletters. (www.loriduffwrites.com) Triple thanks if you ignored all the typos in them because I realized twenty minutes before my self-imposed deadline that I needed to get one out in time.

Thank you to my friends and family who actually seem to like being written about. Thank you to everyone who let me use your real name, and to everyone who helped me pick out a pseudonym.

Thank you to everyone who let me come visit their book club, sell my book at their store, or talk at their event/meeting/etc.

Thank you to my screening committee, Linda and Diane.

Thank you to Anne Finkelman, to whom I do owe a kidney and a cornea as well as several glasses of wine, and whose keen eye for detail caught a great many inconsistencies and typos.

Thank you to Sharon Swanepoel, who not only allows me but continues to encourage me to write for her ever increasing publishing empire.

Thank you for my writing buddies – Skinny Mom and the Dame, and the Post-Patchers. (You know who you are.) Thank you to Suzen Pettit who taught me how to get more than three Twitter followers and how to be famous.

Thank you to the Jew Crew (senior edition) for making me laugh and being my local mishpucha. Let's always spend holidays together.

Even though I said thank you to my family up above, I want to say that again. Specifically my husband, Mike, the boy who won't grow up; Jacob, my boy who won't stop growing; and my ever-quotable daughter, Marin. And a shout out to my parents, Helen and Fred Brudner because quite literally, without the night of joy they had in the waning hours of the 1960's, I would never have been born.

CPSIA information can be obtained
at www.ICGtesting.com
Printed in the USA
LVHW010912290620
659221LV00008B/702